PURPOSE.
POWER.
PERSISTENCE.
PRAYER.

TRINITA R. LATTIMORE, MSC, M.Ed., LGPC, C.C.

ENDORSEMENT by DR. WILLIE JOLLEY

"Trinita Lattimore is a woman who is on a mission…a mission to help people to live more productive lives. She has been through thefires of life and not only survived, but thrived! Read this book andget ready to think different about your possibilities, and also get ready to fly higher!"

Dr. Willie Jolley, CSP, CPAE (Member-Speaker Hall of Fame)

*Named "One of the Outstanding 5 Speakers In The World" - by Toastmasters International

*"Host of the #1 Motivational/ Inspirational Radio Show on Sirius XM!"

* "The Attitude and Achievement Expert"
  We Inspire & Elevate People To Achieve Greater Success

* Best Selling Author of *"A Setback Is A Setup For AComeback"*
  & *"An Attitude of Excellence!"*

* Host of *"The Willie Jolley Show"* on CBS-TV, PBS, Sirius/XM& WHUR-FM

* CBS -TV "Live Better With Willie Jolley"<---click link to view video clip

* **Dr. Willie Jolley - The Impact of Inspiration w/ FordMotors":
  http://bit.ly/1tyJOVh**

* **Willie Jolley Million Dollar Roundtable Sizzle Reel:
  http://vimeo.com/williejolley/mdrtsizzlereel**
  Web: www.williejolley.com / Office: (202) 723-8863

DEDICATION

THIS BOOK IS DEDICATED TO THE LIFE AND MEMORY OF
TWO VERY SPECIAL WOMEN I KNOW I WILL SEE AGAIN.

MY MOM, SONYA E. BALL LATTIMORE RYAN, AND MY
FIRSTCOUSIN, DESIREE JANET LATTIMORE.

YOU ARE BEAUTIFUL...YOUR PURPOSE, POWER,
PERSISTENCEAND PRAYERS...HAVE BEEN FULFILLED.

CONTENTS

ACKNOWLEDGMENTS

*T*o my mother, the late *Sonya B. Ryan,* who always knew that for all those times I ran away, I would come back again someday to fulfill God's purpose for my life. I love you eternally. To all my purpose people...NEVER LET ANYONE RUSH YOUR PURPOSE! I started this book in 1998.

*W*alter L. Lattimore (Daddy Poo) — A Daddy's girl is what I will always think of myself to be. Plus I look just like you. I love you, Daddy Poo!

*K*enny Lattimore (K-boy) — I wish I had waited for love like you no matter what the end result be...lol, but if I did, this book may never have been written, hahaha. With a brother like you, I truly have felt the move of God. Through your gift of song, wisdom, protection, and love, I now know that God has given these gifts to you...because he knew you would surely give it back. I love you for real.

Lauren T. Reynolds (Mamma Wee) — My aunt, a woman who has filled in for the mom I have lost all too soon. You're the best Auntie Wee! Thanks for just being there.

Charles R. Ryan (Chuck) — My stepdad...a man who has stepped up to plate in his own way and impacted my life by surprising me with his unconditional support. God is a healer and God heals relationships.

Pastor Theresa McFaddin — After seeing what God has done in your life, how could I resist following in the footsteps of such a great author, woman, mother, wife and leader. How valuable and resourceful you are, Theresa. Thank you.

Pastor *Jeffrey Boone* — Thank you for the inspiration you gave me to write this book. I shared my assignment and you said, "Trinita, you should write a book." So thanks, for the instruct and inspiration.

Willie Jolly and LaVonia Perryman Fairfax – Two awesome mentors and POWER PEOPLE! Respect goes deep for the two of you. Peace.

****

Last but not least - **To every reader whose life this book will change, encourage and empower...thank you for listening.**

Chapter 1

Kingdom Purpose

Luke 17:21—Neither shall they say, Lo here or Lo there!

For, behold, the kingdom of God is within you.

Where is the Kingdom of God? Is it in some faraway place that we cannot reach? How does this kingdom manifest in your purpose? In this chapter we will provide an answer to all of these questions. As Luke 17 says, the kingdom of God is in you. Granted there is a heavenly place called the kingdom, yet we must remember that the kingdom that is in each of us is a spiritual place. This kingdom comes by way of godly character and power that is founded on biblical kingdom principles.

These principles are manifested within you by what you do and how much you obey them. This kingdom is not in some land of the lost or remote location. This kingdom, praise God, should be evident in the lifestyle of everyone who claims to be a believer. The location of this kingdom is in your heart. The translation of the word *kingdom* means: "Within or among you." Once you acquire an understanding concerning this place called "the kingdom," your purpose will begin to flow with much ease.

Heart knowledge is more important than head knowledge when it comes to the comprehension of your kingdom purpose. This means that although a biblical interpretation can be given to stimulate your thinking, it all starts with a holistic pursuit of kingdom purpose by a personal relationship with God, directly.

No matter where you live in this world, just know that God desires to make a divine connection with you. I believe that as you read this book, a season of release belongs to you. YES, a next level release belongs to YOU!

The scripture interpreted, says that the kingdom of God (heavenly place or spiritually connected) cannot be destroyed or moved. No force of evil can prevail against the kingdom, and nothing can wipe it out. The same goes for you, as you live out the kingdom that is within. No weapon formed will be able to overtake you and prosper, ever! Amen. The exception to this rule is sin. If sin enters into your internal kingdom place, you are headed for a troubled pathway. The kingdom of God (or the kingdom of the Messiah) was grossly misunderstood by the Pharisees.

Luke 17:20a reads, "And when he was demanded of the Pharisees, when the kingdom of God should come, he answered them and said, The kingdom of God cometh not with observation."

See, they had it all wrong in their understanding. They thought the kingdom of God was to come in a tangible or natural earthly way—a visual way.

They were totally oblivious to its actual spiritual purpose within the hearts of men. In order not to fall into the same fleshly misconceptions as the Pharisees did, please be sure to keep in the forefront of your mind that "the kingdom of God is within you." The kingdom of God is a place of total influence via the Spirit of God.

John 18:36—"Jesus answered, 'My kingdom is not of this world: if my kingdom were of this world, then would my servants fight, that I should not be delivered to the Jews: but now is my kingdom not from hence.'"

Do you see my point? The *kingdom of God within* will not change men's outward condition initially, but it will convert their hearts and *then* their lives, if they yield. Don't let the true kingdom pass you by. Don't be ignorant to its true presence, because your purpose as a believer depends on it. Don't you know that your purpose as a believer should closely hold the hand of the kingdom of

God within you? My desire is that we all receive this true revelation and begin to operate in it. Remember, just as the kingdom is eternal, so is your kingdom purpose; it is not temporary, neither should its impact be viewed as a temporary one.

Reward and blessings come with this purpose for the here and now, but especially for the experience and purpose of eternity—the final destination. Now, let's look at some scriptures for proof:

Romans 14:17—"For the kingdom of God is not meat and drink; but righteousness, and peace, and joy in the Holy Ghost."

Luke 10:11—"Even the very dust of your city, which cleaveth on us, we do wipe off against you: notwithstanding be ye sure of this, that the kingdom of God is come nigh (near or to) unto you."

Matthew 12:28—"But if I cast out devils by the Spirit of God, then the kingdom of God is come unto you."

Luke 11:18, 20—"If Satan also be divided against himself, how shall his kingdom stand? Because ye say that I cast out devils through Beelzebub. But if I with the finger of God cast out devils, no doubt the kingdom of God is come upon you."

Luke 13:18–19—"Then said he, Unto what is the kingdom of God like? And whereunto shall I resemble it? It is like a grain of mustard seed, which a man took, and cast into his garden; and it grew, and waxed a great tree; and the fowls of the air lodged in the branches of it."

Do you see my point? Each of these scripturesspeak of a spiritual kingdom and its spiritual effect. Consider *Romans 8:28—"And we know that all things*

work together for good to them that love God, to them

who are the called according to his purpose."

Although this is a familiar passage that many of us have

heard many times over, stop a moment to consider the last

part that declares, "All things will work together for good to

them who are called (*invited*) according to his purpose."

Thank you, Lord, for my kingdom purpose today!

I hope to have brought clarity to your understanding

and desire for kingdom purpose. Kingdom purpose is

God's desire to see his kingdom manifested in you, and

this happens through personal relationship. Listen, there

are many books out there on "purpose," so there is no

excuse. I encourage you to get prepared for your kingdom

purpose!

Read, listen, practice, and expect a perfected and

blessed end result. When Christ died he laid the

foundation and opened up a new way for you to become a

kingdom builder, so let's begin to build. You are obligated

to bear fruit, but if you don't prepare and go forth, fruit will never be birthed and lives will never be impacted for the kingdom of God by YOU!

Consider all that has been invested in you by Christ—your individuality, talents, and gifts as well as God's anointing—and think of what a blessing all of that should be to the kingdom! The question now is: Do you believe it?! I do and that is why I am writing this book to be an encouragement and to show that I too am on the road to preparing for kingdom purpose and fulfillment.

This message is very simple. The work now comes with you making the connection for your life.

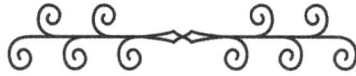

Pray This Prayer for Your Kingdom Purpose

Jesus, I thank you for helping me to realize my kingdom purpose. I want to build a personal relationship with you here on Earth before going back to my heavenly home in glory. Father, please bless me as I now take your desire for kingdom purpose within me and allow its manifestation in my life.

Father, may you be pleased with my submission to your Holy Spirit. May my kingdom purpose not only be a blessing to the reputation of God but to those who witness it through my life. I know this journey will come with challenges, but Father, I trust your all-controlling divine plan and purpose for my life. In Jesus' name I pray. Amen.

Chapter 2

Life without Power —
I'm Thirsty

Revelation 21:6—*"And he said unto me, It is done. I am Alpha and Omega, the beginning and the end. I will give unto him that is athirst of the fountain of the water of life freely."*

What would life be without a godly power? Who would you be without a godly power or power at all? The world is filled with billions of people from various walks of life. What real significance would the lives of each individual hold, if they did not serve in some powerful capacity? Everywhere you turn, you will find a man, a woman, a boy, or a girl living their lives as it has been designed or predestined for them to live.

Man has built for himself a world, where God has allowed him some control and complete dominion.

Schools have been constructed, businesses have been developed, dreams have been realized, and goals have been achieved. But what has God really created you for? Why are you really here? What is your life's purpose and the power you have to make it happen? You may have traveled and seen some of the world or even all of it, but what is it all for, if at the end of the day you have impacted no one and not made a difference in anyone's life? Maybe you have only been as far as your own backyard or city block. Is this all there is for you? Is where you are today, all that God has for your life and for your existence and the power you have within?

I know these are a lot of questions, but in order to get to the answers, you must first ask questions. While some may have their own philosophies concerning the answer, the most important question to ask in your search for life's power and purpose is this: How can I know for sure who I am and who God is or should be in my life and purpose? Is there any real proof that God has empowered me?

The answer to all of the above questions will be revealed. Let's look at this proof through the written word of God. Why was I born? Why will I die? Why am I the race that I am? Why do I believe the way I do? Is there a reason that I was born into a poor family or a rich one? Is my life without power and purpose? The answer to all of these questions is found in what is called the Bible.

The Bible is the inspired, infallible, and immutable written word of God. God has given the gift of how to live a life of godly purpose in the format of sixty-six books. From Genesis to Revelation, he has expressed, expounded, instructed, warned, explained, and enlightened. The bottom line is whosoever will take heed from listening and really get the message should simply...get with the program.

He even goes as far as sending his only begotten son, who is the Word incarnate (which means the Word of God in human form). The word does more·than give us clues and implications; the Word gives us clear-cut direction and absolute truth, and it supplies help in our lives every day. The Lord's purpose for us is in the here and now, the future, and even in our past experiences. He will brilliantly paint for us a picture that could only be designed by his omniscient hand.

Yes, believe it or not, the higher power is God, and He is able! Well, since I am living in the right now...the "Rhema" (right now or present) word," and instruction for my life is to live with power...and to be absolutely powerful.

Once you understand this plan for the place of power in your life, you may wonder what your power means and how you can ensure you don't miss God's divine place of power for you. Here's the starting point:

You must make up your mind that the written word is going to be your absolute dependence and guide. For every question, every concern, and every care, the written word is there to guide you. Let this truth be your conviction.

One thing that every person can be sure of, is that God has created us all and the end result of that creation is to bring Himself glory. God has glorified, justified, and sanctified the believer.

This glorification, justification, and sanctification only belong to those who have accepted Christ as their personal Lord and Savior. This is the realization of the starting point, and the first step in your answer toward understanding the deep roots of a powerful foundation. But let's go deeper. Remember, we are digging for foundational answers to life's power for you…right now!

Once you become a true Christian (I mean Chris-like and sold out), you may ask, what is this glorified, justified, and sanctified state of being? The answer goes like this: **glorified** means to be made better, larger; and finer than is actually the case; **justified** means to be freed from blame, to be declared guiltless; **sanctified** means to be made holy and set apart, free from sin and purified.

So now, let's look at the written word and examine how God actually does this glorifying, justifying, and sanctifying.

First we'll look at glorified. *Romans 8:29–30 says, "For whom he did foreknow, he also did predestinate to be conformed to the image of his Son, that hemight be the firstborn among many brethren. Moreover whom he did predestinate, them he alsocalled: and whom he called, them he also justified:and whom he justified, them he also glorified."*

Every man, woman, boy, and girl is called to salvation by the loving and merciful outstretched hand of God. He called you to be conformed, or changed. This is his first act of power for you—to be a changed and powerful person. Because he knew that your original state from birth was one of imperfection, he sent his only begotten son, Jesus Christ by name, to help you to acquire this change in your life. After providing the free gift of salvation through his son, he brought about an even deeper blessing and that blessing was to take the wretched state that you and I were born into, and glorifying, justifying, and sanctifying us by his omnipotent power. *I Corinthians 6:20 says, "For ye are bought with a price: therefore glorify God in your body, and in your spirit which are God's."* **For that reason** we should no longer do the things that we used to do. We should allow the purpose that has been given to come to a complete manifestation in ourselves in order that he who has created us will be well pleased.

Now, let's look at justifying. Titus 3:4–7 says, *"But after that the kindness and love of God our*

Saviour toward man appeared, Not by works of righteousness which we have done, but according to his mercy he saved us, by the washing of regeneration, and renewing of the Holy Ghost; Which he shed on us abundantly through Jesus Christ our Saviour; That being justified by his grace, we should be made heirs according to the hope of eternal life.

As undeserving as we are, God himself says to his creation, to his people of power. "Yes, I see the end result for you and you cannot work for my grace, for my grace is the unmerited (*undeserved*), love and favor I have toward you." In other words, he gives it to you and me for free! So true this is that while we work to gain education, meet career goals, and raise families, the one thing that should be most significant of all is the grace of God, and, remember, no man can work for that. Amen.

Justified by his grace is so awesome because it means that though we did not deserve it, he took our blame and made us blameless, and he took our guilt and made us guiltless. Case dismissed. We are saved byGod's wonderful grace, Amen!

Let's look at sanctifying. *I Corinthians 6:9–11 says, "Know ye not that the unrighteous shall notinherit the kingdom of God? Be not deceived neither fornicators, nor idolaters, nor adulterers, nor effeminate, nor abusers of themselves with mankind, Nor thieves, nor covetous, nor drunkards, nor revilers, nor extortioners, shall inherit the kingdom of God. And such were some of you: but ye are washed, but ye are sanctified, but ye are justified in the name of the Lord Jesus, and by the Spirit of our God."*

By his Spirit, by his power, and by his might are we sanctified, holy, set apart and made clean by his blood. Clean from what? Clean from the scars of sin. Listen, God has plans for your life, do you believe it? Because of his power, he has freed us from those things we used to do. He washed my sins away through the power of his blood. Our old ways—self-medication, alcohol consumption, bad eating, corrupt and profane speech, and especially ways of thinking—must die. Amen. Now we can walk in this newness of life, breathe in this newness of life, and even find peaceful rest in this newness of life! Don't fall back on the excuse of everything being just a process.

Sometimes God wants us to participate by doing the work. Work is work, and it is not just a process of going through the motions—amen? But in the end you are rewarded when it's time to rest from work. Unfortunately, the work may be hard and self-sacrifice may be involved, but at the end is the power displayed, fulfilled, the dream come true, and the prayer answered.

You and I know that life can make you feel like you are in a choke hold. Sometimes you feel that you can't breathe or find peace. Why? Because sometimes we have so many concerns, and we can become overwhelmed with expectations and irritated due to the long waiting periods of God.

But I've got good news for you, because of Christ we can live our lives with powerful expectation and not expect in vain! If the Lord saw fit to do all of the above, then we should know that before we leave this earth, whether by death or by rapture (*rapture* means "caught up"), our powerful influences will be fulfilled.

God will not allow us to have the testimony of a life without a true connection to power. Do you believe it? I do. So, no matter where you are today and no matter what you may be going through, find the Lord Jesus. Pray the prayer of salvation admitting your state of sin and need of a deliverer from that place of wrong and sin. Believe in your heart and confess with your mouth that Jesus Christ is the Lord to the glory of God.

As Romans 10:9–10 says, "For if you confess with your mouth that Jesus is Lord and believe in your heart that God raised him from the dead, you will be saved. For it is by believing in your heart that you are made right with God, and it is by confessing with your mouth that you are saved."

All of the answers to your very being found are in the written word of God because the Word brings victory! The enemy cannot keep you ignorant of your victory once you have found the truth, and the truth lies in God's word. To some, this is controversial, I know, but the Word is the resource of truth, and the foundation for this book.

Genesis 1:26–27 says, "And God said, Let us make man in our image, after our likeness: and let them have dominion over the fish of the sea, and over the fowl of the air and over the cattle, and over all the earth, and over every creeping thing that creepeth upon the earth. So God created man in his own image, in the image of God created he him; male and female created he them."

As we see in the scripture, God gave man the power to have dominion over all; we have been created in the image of God. This is nothing to take lightly; it says that the enemy has nothing because God gave us everything.

John 10:10 says, "The thief cometh not, but for to steal, and to kill, and to destroy: I am come that they might have life, and that they might have it more abundantly." Although Satan comes to steal, kill and destroy, he is still defeated and God's end result for you and I is VICTORY—with a life of power, purpose and abundance.

The word of God teaches us how to use the Word as a powerful weapon against defeat, depression, discouragement, oppression, and so forth. To experience a life with power, we must apply the Word to the places in ourselves that are not yielding to the Holy Spirit. Call on the name of Jesus, and be an effective witness (once you are born again) and God will begin to build upon you spiritually.

As a result, your testimony about what he has done for you will become so much more effective. Always know that the scriptures are the proof of what God has created you to be. Have the confidence and see the end result.

Psalm 8:4–7 says, "What is man, that thou art mindful of him? And the son of man, that thou visitest him? For thou hast made him a little lower than the angels, and has crowned him with glory and honor. Thou madest him to have dominion over the works of thy hands: thou hast put all things under his feet: All sheep and oxen, yea and the beasts of the field; the fowl of the air, and the fish of the sea, and whatsoever passeth through the paths of the seas."

Look at all we have: he visits us; he thinks about us; he has crowned us with glory; he has crowned us with honor; he has given us dominion and put all things under our feet. Amen. Now with all of this power given freely to us, why do people seek power from people, money, or in other ways and things? Seeking out power can cause great problems. Not all people are ungodly power seekers, but for those of you who are, and are reading this book by God's ordained purpose, this forewarning simply means, let go and let God. Death has no place in your place of power, for all things are given to you freely.

Addictions have no place in your place of power, for all things are given to you freely and with responsibility— by God's divine authority! Sexual immorality has no place in your purpose, for all things are given to you freely. Being disobedient to parents has no place in your purpose, for all things are given to you freely. Husbands and wives, there is no place for the enemy in your marriage, for all things are given to you freely. God made you one in marriage because that is what he wanted marriage to represent: oneness. Hunger and thirst for God's best and the best from God will come to you.

Young people, there is no need to be in a frustrated position in life, because God has given to you freely. Respect your parents so that your life will be long and blessed. Walk in that freedom today.

All of us should hunger to be in the most intimate and holy place with him. This simply means being in his presence, sharing with him, hearing from him, getting to know him better, building a friendship with the Lord, becoming more intimate (meaning close) with him. As of today, you must tell yourself that your life does have power and you will make it! No matter what is going on in your family, in your work, in school, or even in the world, you can be strong and powerful in your mind.

God is protecting you and will protect you for your life's purpose. Stand if that is all you can do, just stand even if you do not have a dime in your pocket or a friend in the world. Pray to the Almighty El Shaddai, which means "the Lord God Almighty," and believe him for your tomorrow as well as for your today.

The closeness of a man with a woman is a closeness of the flesh, but to experience the closeness of the Lord is more intimate than the flesh, for it is one with the Spirit. It is very special and unique. A spiritual closeness with the Lord is essential in your life's place of power because no matter what anyone may say to you or about you, your relationship with the Lord will make you strong and confident...POWERFUL!

This happens through what God's Spirit and Word says about who you are. On a daily basis we can be discouraged and under attack, or at least feel that way. Challenges come, but God provides strength. Remember that God's intends for you to give him the glory, so just be willing to do it through whatever life may bring—whether crisis or celebration! Wipe away tears and expect.

The Bible declares in a few scriptures that power is real and it's effects shall come to pass. Here are some of those scriptures to encourage you:

- **Ephesians 3:20** – "Now unto him that is able to do exceeding abundantly above all that we ask or think, according to the power that worketh in us,..."

- **1 Corinthians 6:14** - And God hath both raised up the Lord, and will also raise up us by his own power.

- **1 Corinthians 4:20** - For the kingdom of God [is] not in word, but in power.

- **Ephesians 6:10** - Finally, my brethren, be strong in the Lord, and in the power of his might.

I love the scriptures because they say to me that God is in control and no one can remove, stop, hinder, or change (disannul) his power or his purpose. Nations, nor the whole earth, can deter whatever he deems for you and for me. Just know that it shall come to pass, no matter where you live or what government you are under. Everything has been made manifested to us by God through Jesus Christ which is all in his powerful hand.

In my last point, I wish to propose the question of a powerful life? What is the intent of your life and are you sure of the power inside of you given by God? If your answer is YES and you know the intent of your power, then you are doing real well. You are on your way. Act on it. If your answer is NO, then I pray that after reading this book, you will seek the Lord for salvation. Developing a relationship with him that from this day forward, his power and will for your life will be made very clear to you and you will begin to operate in it. May the Lord get all of the glory that is due his matchless name, in his divine power for YOU!

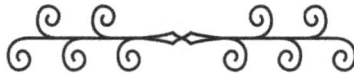

***

Pray This Prayer for Life's Power

Lord, I come to you with my life ready to be placed in your hand. Bless me because of your greatness and my faith in you for my life's great purpose. Bless me in my walk, talk, and especially in my living before you. Bless me in my life's destiny and give me the power and strength I need. Multiply and increase me more and more. You are my life, my King, my Lord! I truly turn over my whole life and self to you. In Jesus' name I pray. Amen! Please keep me in your powerful hand.

Chapter 3

A Man's Purpose and Persistence

Genesis 5:1-2—*This is the book of the generations of Adam. In the day that God created man, in the likeness of God made he him; Male and female created he them; and blessed them, and called their name Adam, in the day when they were created.* (John Wesley's Explanatory Notes)

A man with a persistence is awesome, but, a man with a perfected persistence is even better than that! This chapter may be a little controversial to some and I am aware of that, but please read it with an open mind and an open heart and understand the intention that I have in writing about such a sensitive area. The content that this chapter will cover will be encouraging but may also feel like chastisement. Yet my goal in writing it is to hopefully enlighten the ones who have been given a very special gift from God called headship and leadership.

Men, do you know how powerful you are? Do you know that although there may be some heavy-hitting negatives that surround some of the things you do or have done, you must still be persistent?   The bottom line is that you are great. Women love you., and children love and need you. A real man is priceless and takes responsibility, and this is what I personally believe about men.

As you read this chapter, open yourself up to receive and take on the responsibilities. Although you may not have asked for it, just know that because of your position in creation, you are to be the persistent, responsible owners of it. I call it "**Man Purpose and Persistence.**"

You are a man, created in the direct image of God. You are powerful, and you were created cause God had thoughts of you...yes you. First of all, I would like to say that I am writing this chapter to the men. I want you to know that I hear very loudly glass crashing complaints against you. The glass has been broken, and shattered glass is left crushed on the ground of expectation and faced with disappointment, where some, even most of you are concerned.

This is why I am going to do something that is out of my own comfort zone...confront. Yes, this chapter will help men perfect their persistence for change, by confrontation. In the end, my goal is to hopefully cause men to celebrate themselves as they perfect their own persistence toward change. Where men are concerned, I have great empathy but anger too. I have three brothers. They are very different and unique. I know a little of each one's personality and I have observed how their lives have turned out.

One is very successful and has dealt with his success and the struggles with the grace of God and his decision to hold fast to the leading of the Holy Spirit. Another has dealt with childhood traumas with the loss of his mother at an early age and dropping out of school, yet going back and achieving his educational goal with persistence and accomplishment. Now married with children and a loving caregiver or dogs, (especially pit bulls). The other has found a loving wife and become a husband and father and an overall persistent and independent leader by self-determination. My father is awesome although he has faced many challenges in his life. He is not perfect and neither was his father before him, but they were the patriarchs of the family and that can never be stripped from them no matter what. My dad was successful at persistence and in attempting to be himself and in working a job until the age of retirement. He had seven children and he fulfilled his life's purpose to travel and dream—he loves South Africa. These are my men. They are not perfect, but they are purpose filled, powerful and persistent. Where men are concerned, I again have some levels of empathy and anger combined. Especially with those in my culture.

Yet, in spite of myself, I desire to expose men to something other than the hidden agenda of pardoning and patronizing. I believe that women and men can understand each other and get along.

Yes, the heterosexual male and female are at odds most of the time, but I believe that as we all step up to the plate and persistently pursue change…change will happen. It will take some work but there is a reward in the end. If you are a man who desires to walk with persistence, please know that it does not mean you are to be 100 percent perfect upfront. No, perfecting anything takes time, as you surely know.

I do believe that you can walk in your persistence toward change and work on making it better, one small or giant step at a time. It depends on you. Now, my anger stems from the feelings that some men have had in wanting to throw in the towel of life and give up; please note I said "some" men. Hello, my brothers! Giving up is not the step to take.

Giving up on your ability to provide for your family is not the step to take; the same goes for giving up on finding a job...and keeping one. Men must keep themselves spiritually connected to God and self. A man that gives up is not a very strong man. But he can be! Allowing persistence to come alive in you is key. Be persistent and walk in wisdom. Never allow yourselves to be abused and being abusive (victims and abusers of domestic violence) because this is not who God called you to be.

Do you really know who you are today? Have you man of persistent purpose, been persistent in finding yourselves? As you strive, push, press, cry, fight spiritually, and feel anger, be sure to stop for a moment and be able to listen! Listen to the money you have to invest—is it enough? Listen to the woman or women in your lives—what do they say? Listen to the voice of God— what is he saying. Listen to the other men who mean you well—what do they say? Listen to yourself too—what are you saying? The reason for all of this listening is for direction, healing, victory, purpose, and fulfillment! Yes, you can have it all as a man, so, be persistent in who God has called you to be*!*

Habakkuk 2:2 says, "And the LORD answered me, and said, 'Write the vision, and make it plain upon tables, that he may run that readeth it.'"

What's my point? My point is that a man with a perfected and persistent-powerful purpose...listens.

Although God has anointed the man in a way that he has not anointed a woman, listening does not cost you anything. Investigate, ask questions, and wait on the Lord for your decision-making direction.

God speaks through people, and he speaks divinely through the Holy Spirit. Your perfected persistence needs you to do more than just survive. A perfected persistence in a man rises to the forefront when he knows who he is. Who does God say you are? His desires and his plans for your life start with a personal relationship with him. Yes, with who he is in your life?

There is so much that a man with a purpose and persistence needs to know, but all will be revealed, so just take one step at a time. It depends on you and your persistence as a man. Go after it and go for it! Whatever it be that's righteous and good.

I Corinthians 2:9–10 says, "But as it is written, Eye hath not seen, nor ear heard, neither have entered into the heart of man, the things which God hath prepared for them that love him. But God hath revealed them unto us by his Spirit: for the Spirit searcheth all things, yea, the deep things of God."

Even though so much expectation has been placed on the man, the final goal is for you, man, to be prepared and to take the steps that yield only successful godliness and holiness. That is the structure for a godly foundation.

Hello men! In order to perfect the uncovered persistent in you, you must, let the relationship with the one who created you be perfected. It starts with knowledge and understanding of who God is to you.

God can make you into the greatest man you can be, and that starts with being a man of surrender. Humble yourself, because although the male ego is an important created structure of the man, a strong base in spiritual character and development, is essential to his moving forward.

By behavioral science interpretation, the ego is the balance of the desire to please the self (id) and being all about the morals only (super ego), but God called men to be sober and balanced, from a religious and spiritual perspective. He's called you to be persistent and to lead and love via your own submission to God and man (woman). Love people into submission…stop demanding it…it will come. Be persistent you can have it all!

What is the scripture instructing? It is instructing you to be sober. Ask King Solomon what happens when you don't walk in sobriety. Read I Samuel 15 to learn about that.

In short, a man who follows God's instruction is a man that is surely headed toward his perfected place via persistence. Let's face it. God has expectations for your purpose-filled, powerful and persistent life. Going along to get along is not living in persistence.

You can and must do more. Explore, ask, observe, and model the character of God and other legally successful men. This is the bottom line and responsibility of the man of a perfected purpose: Be sober, sold out, Spirit led, strong, saved, stable, smart, salaried, and sensitive. Here's the thing, you can't do it without persistence.

Personally, I didn't grow up with the most positive feelings about men, but because of the grace of God, I am now willing and able to show men the level of respect that God has given to them as the head.

Respect really is a two-way street but men you must respect you, first. Men and women must respect each other as human beings, created special in God. Men you can lead a woman but not with a selfish agenda. After awhile you could find yourself alone and by yourself and that defeats relationships, of all types.

This is why it is good for a man to find a partner. God created it to be so, but if that has not happened for you as a man, it's okay, because not everyone marries. Don't be intimidated by women who are powerful in places that God has called them to walk. You are still the man and should need no validation. Walk in Man Purpose-Persistence and don't build relationships sexually outside of the way God created it to be, because that could be a challenge to you living a fruitful life.

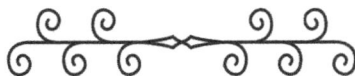

Pray This Prayer for a Man's Purpose

God, I am a man and I was created by you in your image. Help me to be the man you want me to be. Give me the strength to lead, love, serve, and be

sensitive to the leading of your word and your Spirit. Bless me and all the men who stand unmoved, valiant, and mighty in being persistent. Without your power and guidance, where would I be? Oh God, you are my strength and helper. Please touch my life and heal me where I have been broken and shut down. Remove anger and challenges from my past. Move me upward and forward as I desire to be the man you have created me to be. In Jesus' name. Amen.

Chapter 4

A Woman's Purpose

Exodus 15:20—*Then Miriam the prophet, Aaron's sister, took a tambourine and led all the women in rhythm and dance.*

What is a woman of a divine purpose made of? Is it sugar, spice, and everything nice as the old nursery rhyme states? What does it mean to be divine in a purpose? To find the answer to these two questions I began to do some research and soul-searching.

The dictionary defines the word *divine* as **"of or like God or a god; given or inspired by God; holy; sacred; devoted to God."** [1] **(Webster's dictionary.com).**

Being saved for many years, I began to ponder whether I was the best woman that I could be in God's prescribed plan according to Proverbs 31.

Was I really a Proverbs 31 woman? Looking at things from a spiritual standpoint, I knew I needed to do some soul searching and self-examination. But where would I start? I began to seek the Lord for the right place and the book of Galatians came to mind.

Galatians 5:22 says, "But the fruit of the Spirit is love, joy, peace, longsuffering, gentleness, goodness, faith, meekness, temperance: against such there is no law."

Bingo! Why not start with the fruit of the Spirit? Showing the fruit was an area for me that needed consistency; it was time for that journey to begin.

Romans 12:1 says, "I beseech you therefore brethren, by the mercies of God that ye present your bodies a living sacrifice, holy, acceptable unto God, which is your reasonable service."

Remember, woman of divine and perfected purpose, everything starts with you and your Bible-based, Spirit-led convictions. Make decisions to be like Christ. It's not a hard thing (if you are a true believer), but it does require you to make up your mind and be determined.

Just ask yourself this question: "Is my attitude about people, situations, and circumstances what God wants it to be?"

It does not always feel good to admit our wrongs. Sometimes we prefer to use excuses to protect ourselves. We all go down that street sometimes. Instead of humbly admitting our faults and needs, we live in denial. llowing the character of Christ through the Holy Spirit to shine through should be a major step in the divine and perfected "YOU."

Philippians 2:5 says, "Let this mind be in you, which was also in Christ Jesus."

As women we can hold on to so much stuff— unnecessary stuff—you feel me? To handle this I had to stop the train of life and ask myself if I was ready to humble myself, slow down, and love unconditionally. Listen woman of divine and perfected purpose, it's time to "shake loose!" Release yourself from yourself and cling to Christ. You can do it. Trust me. Cognitive changes yield behavioral changes.

As I began to observe my own personal behavior and growth, I saw that I really needed to pray about myself more and apply the scriptures.

When in doubt of how I was to react to a certain situation or to someone's behavior, the first thing I had to do was to admit to myself that I really wanted to please God. Allowing God to help me focus and put all things into the right perspective spiritually was a giant leap forward for me. I started putting it ALL in his hands.

I often feel compelled to do things my own way, but I have to keep learning to allow God to put things in place for me. I have to ask myself whether my decisions are for me or whether they are going to be God's. Was it going to be my way or his way? My aim and long-term goal was to be a purpose-filled woman who was no longer her own. I knew that I had been purchased by God and that I was all of what he had invested in me.

He is my personal Lord and my Savior who now holds me accountable as to how I carry myself as a divine woman of perfected purpose. Whenever my flesh would rise up, I knew how to humble myself and behave myself in his righteousness. When problems arose or if I felt like I was in a slump or a mood, I began to thank him, deny myself, read the Word, fast, praise him, worship him totally, release myself to him, and expect him to meet me right there in that place of need. And, he did.

My prayer for all women is to realize their divine purpose and to walk in a divine capacity of godly self-empowerment to the glory of God. That is not always easy to do, but I encourage you to fight for it—fight for the right. By that I mean fight spiritually for the righteous character of

Christ. You and I can do this. Now at other times, I felt like giving up, and you will probably feel that way too.

Yet even when I felt like giving up, divine purpose—yes, Woman purpose—was calling me hard. A good question to ask yourself and one that I have asked is whether you can go forth in your perfected purpose without God being absolutely first. I knew the steps to take but I had to ask myself if God was really first in my life. It is very important to evaluate that area. How could any woman love, serve, and obey God and go forth with purpose without yielding to the almighty God, first?

Jesus must be all in all for you personally. To every woman of divine purpose, I admonish you to examine yourselves. Take the time needed to get to know God and to allow him to know you, for he in turn will show you the "real you." It's good to go off and be alone and just take that much needed quiet time—just for you.

I hear some women say they just need some "me time." But remember that as you take that time to be sure to include God time. A nice hotel room in an expensive or inexpensive place with a hot tub or just a nice bathtub may be good for the mind and relaxing to the body, but make that Spirit man a priority.

Know him as Jehovah-Raphe (my Healer), **Jehovah-Shalom** (my Peace), and **Jehovah-Jireh** (my Provider). Take the steps to really make him the lover of your soul, and make sure your soul loves Him back. For if your soul does not truly love Him back, then your whole purpose as a woman of God will remain empty and void. To be an effective woman of divine and perfected purpose in Christ means to be a woman sold out for everything that God has assigned and gifted her to be. Keep your focus and be balanced.

If you are a married woman with children, your focus and main purpose must be toward God first and then your family. Sometimes you have to minister to your household first before running the house of the Lord. If you are not married, your focus and main purpose will and should be toward God first, yourselves, and then others.

Woman of purpose, be a profound woman of divine and perfected purpose. Be a fearless woman of divine and perfected purpose. Be a strong woman of divine and perfected purpose. Be an honest woman of divine and perfected purpose. Be a joyful woman of divine and perfected purpose. Be a peaceful woman of divine and perfected purpose. Be a gentle woman of divine and perfected purpose. Be a good woman of divine and perfected purpose. Be a giving woman of divine and perfected purpose. Be a meek woman of divine and perfected purpose. Finally, be a temperate woman of divine and perfected purpose.

Above all, be a woman of obedience and watch the blessings flow right into your purpose and your life. To all of my sisters in the faith, and for those who are yet to come, Ephesians 6:10 says, *"Be strong in the lord and in the power of his might." Amen.*

Proverbs 31:10-31

- Who can find a virtuous woman? For her price is far above rubies.

-The heart of her husband doth safely trust in her, so that he shall have no need of spoil.

-She will do him good and not evil all the days of her life.

-She seeketh wool, and flax and worketh willingly with her hands.

-She is like the merchants' ships; she bringeth her food from afar.

-She riseth also while it is yet night, and giveth meat to her household, and a portion to her maidens.

-She considereth a field, and buyeth it: with the fruit of her hands she planteth a vineyard.

-She girdeth her loins with strength, and strengtheneth her arms. (She exercises).

-She perceiveth that her merchandise is good: her hands hold the distaff.

-She stretcheth out her hand to the poor; yea she reacheth for forth her hands to the needy.

-She is not afraid of the snow for her household: for all her household are clothed with scarlet.

-She maketh herself coverings of tapestry; her clothing is silk and purple.

-Her husband is known in the gates, when he sitteth among the elders of the land.

-She maketh fine linen, and selleth it; and delivereth girdles unto the merchant.

-Strength and honour are her clothing; and she shall rejoice in time to come.

-She openeth her mouth with wisdom; and in her tongue is the law of kindness.

-She looketh well to the ways of her household, and eateth not the bread of idleness.

-Her children arise up and call her blessed; her husband also and he praiseth her.

-Many daughters have done virtuously, but thou excellest them all.

-Favour is deceitful, and beauty is vain: but a woman that feareth the Lord, she shall be praised.

-Give her of the fruit of her hands; and her own works shall praise her in the gates.

Pray This Prayer to Be a Woman of Divine and Perfected Purpose

Lord, I praise you and bow down before you. I praise and love you, oh mighty King. I worship you! Thank you for calling me and using a woman like me I am who I am because of you. Help me to continue to seek your face in my divine and perfected purpose as a woman. Just keep me close to you. Whether I preach, teach, sing, live, laugh, cry, give, smile, or frown, may the enemy never, ever be able to pull me away from your joy and your purpose! In Jesus' name I pray. Amen.

Chapter 5

Jump Start Purpose with Prayer

Ecclesiastes 8:6—*"Because to every purpose there is time and judgment, therefore the misery of man is great upon him."*

In order to approach this very sensitive area of your purpose, I thought to use the scripture from ***Ecclesiastes 8:6a*. The Matthew Henry Commentary says*: *"All the events concerning us, with the exact time of them, are determined and appointed in the counsel and foreknowledge of God, and all in wisdom: To every purpose there is a time prefixed, and it is the best time, for it is time and judgment, time appointed both in wisdom and righteousness; the appointment is not chargeable with folly or iniquity" (Henry, M. Complete Commentary 1706).*

The way I read this commentary, I see that foolishness and sin cannot have a place in your purpose for it is the wisdom of God and his righteous that allow the perfection of—the best time for—our purposes. This means we must pray about it. Seeing, talking, and listening are the sure signs of excellence in any realm of communication. I would always say to my students in the classroom that in order for you to succeed in class, on a job, and socially, you must be able to exercise your listening and speaking skills.

God is the director and we are to pray and to follow his directions. He speaks to us, and we speak back to him. We pray to him and he answers our prayers and whether it is what we want to hear or not, this is the way we are to do it. It works, and throughout the Bible you will see how wonderful it is. Let's look at the story of Gideon's purpose for a minute In *Judges 6:11-39:*

And there came an angel of the LORD, and sat under an oak which was in Ophrah, that pertained unto Joash the Abiezrite: and his son Gideon threshed wheat by the winepress, to hide it from the Midianites. And the angel of the LORD appeared unto him, and said unto him, "The LORD is with thee, thou mighty man of valour." And Gideon said unto him, "Oh my Lord, if the LORD be with us, why then is all this befallen us? and where be all his miracles which our fathers told us of, saying, 'Did not the LORD bring us up from Egypt?' but now the LORD hath forsaken us, and delivered us into the hands of the Midianites." And the LORD looked upon him, and said, "Go in this thy might, and thou shalt save Israel from the hand of the Midianites: have not I sent thee?" And he said unto him, "Oh my Lord, wherewith shall I save Israel? behold, my family is poor in Manasseh, and I am the least in my father's house." And the LORD said unto him, "Surely I will be with thee, and thou shalt smite the Midianites as one

man." And he said unto him, "If now I have found

grace in thy sight, then shew me a sign that thou

talkest with me. Depart not hence, I pray thee, until I

come unto thee, and bring forth my present, and set it

before thee." And he said, "I will tarry until thou come

again." And Gideon went in, and made ready a kid,

and unleavened cakes of an ephah of flour: the flesh

he put in a basket, and he put the broth in a pot, and

brought it out unto him under the oak, and presented

it. And the angel of God said unto him, "Take the flesh

and the unleavened cakes, and lay them upon this

rock, and pour out the broth." And he did so. Then the

angel of the LORD put forth the end of the staff that was

in his hand, and touched the flesh and the unleavened

cakes; and there rose up fire out of the rock, and

consumed the flesh and the unleavened cakes. Then

the angel of the LORD departed out of his sight. And

when Gideon perceived that he was an angel of the

LORD, Gideon said, "Alas, O LORD God! for because I

have seen an angel of the LORD face to face." 23 *And*

the LORD said unto him, "Peace be unto thee; fear not:

thou shalt not die." Then Gideon built an altar there

unto the LORD, and called it Jehovahshalom: unto this

day it is yet in Ophrah of the Abiezrites. And it came

to pass the same night, that the LORD said unto him,

"Take thy father's young bullock, even the second

bullock of seven years old, and throw down the altar of

Baal that thy father hath, and cut down the grove that

is by it: 26 *And build an altar unto the LORD thy God*

upon the top of this rock, in the ordered place, and

take the second bullock, and offer a burnt sacrifice

with the wood of the grove which thou shalt cut

down." Then Gideon took ten men of his servants, and

did as the LORD had said unto him: and so it was,

because he feared his father's household, and the men

of the city, that he could not do it by day, that he did it by night. And when the men of the city arose early in the morning, behold, the altar of Baal was cast down, and the grove was cut down that was by it, and the second bullock was offered upon the altar that was built. And they said one to another, Who hath done this thing? And when they enquired and asked, they said, "Gideon the son of Joash hath done this thing." Then the men of the city said unto Joash, "Bring out thy son, that he may die: because he hath cast down the altar of Baal, and because he hath cut down the grove that was by it." And Joash said unto all that stood against him, "Will ye plead for Baal? will ye save him? he that will plead for him, let him be put to death whilst it is yet morning: if he be a god, let him plead for himself, because one hath cast down his altar." Therefore on that day he called him Jerubbaal, saying, "Let Baal plead against him, because he hath thrown down his altar." Then all the Midianites and the

Amalekites and the children of the east were gathered

together, and went over, and pitched in the valley of

Jezreel. But the Spirit of the LORD came upon Gideon,

and he blew a trumpet; and Abiezer was gathered after

him. And he sent messengers throughout all

Manasseh; who also was gathered after him: and he

sent messengers unto Asher, and unto Zebulun, and

unto Naphtali; and they came up to meet them. [36] *And*

Gideon said unto God, "If thou wilt save Israel by mine

hand, as thou hast said, [37] *Behold, I will put a fleece of*

wool in the floor; and if the dew be on the fleece only,

and it be dry upon all the earth beside, then shall I

know that thou wilt save Israel by mine hand, as thou

hast said." And it was so: for he rose up early on the

morrow, and thrust the fleece together, and wringed

the dew out of the fleece, a bowl full of water. [39] *And*

Gideon said unto God, "Let not thine anger be hot

against me, and I will speak but this once: let me prove, I pray thee, but this once with the fleece; let it now be dry only upon the fleece, and upon all the ground let there be dew."

What this says to me is that a lot of times we pray and ask questions, seeking God's guidance and direction for our purposes, yet when the answer comes we struggle with it. What baffles me is that if you pray about a specific purpose, is God not able to prepare you for it? Are our prayers not powerful enough to reach and touch the heart of God? Especially, if your purpose is to bring to Him the glory! Amen!

Sometime we are like Gideon in our preparation for our purpose. We pray and we understand the power of our prayers because we understand the power of God, but we still sometimes just don't pray hard enough and believe long enough, meaning we are not consistent in our prayer life and we don't want to wait. I know this because I was one of those who didn't pray hard enough and believe long enough. Be a people of prayer. Let's not play games with our purpose.

Get ready...pray...listen...and wait. I am preaching to myself right now! Realize also that by preparing for your purpose through prayer, you are affecting the lives of others. Look at all of those who were affected by Gideon's obedience when Gideon was instructed by the Angel of the Lord, and how he not only heard but listened, which brought about the blessing and affected all.

Ask questions. God is not afraid to answer them. If you are not sure, it is your job to pray for clarity and God's choice to release it. You have probably heard it said that God is omniscient, which means is he is all knowing. Yes, he is all knowing and doesn't mind answering what we may think are dumb questions. Remember, God is not like people; there is no arrogance in God.. In order for us to do what he wants, we must step out of the box of fear or doubt and pray and believe. Then pray and believe some more!

When I was growing up, I was always taught to ask for something. I wasn't permitted to just go take it. You were probably taught the same thing as a child. The point to the lesson is simple: You MUST ask. Remembering this lesson, I can easily transition into what God wants from me—which is to just ask him. When you give your life to Christ, from that moment on God will be in control of your purpose. How much control you give him is predicated upon your relationship with him and whatever he directs your path in life to be. Is your purpose to be financially stable? To be healed? To be a college graduate? To be married? To have a wonderful job? To have a child? These are desires that God places in us as his creation: Yes, YOU are his creation.

You were God's idea. Everything about you He created. So, you can't be judged or condemned, because you only belong to God and not man. Let me back this up with a scripture.

Isaiah 54:17 says, "No weapon that is formed against thee shall prosper; and every tongue that shall rise against thee in judgment thou shalt condemn. This is the heritage of the servants of the LORD, and their righteousness is of me, saith the LORD."

In other words, what is right and/or wrong for you is not to be determined by those who try to condemn you, but is to be determined by the Lord! Now, this does not mean that you do not have a responsibility to be right and penitent if necessary; it simple means no one else is better than you. *Romans 3:23 says, "For all have sinned, and come short of the glory of God."*

Look at Saul for instance:

I Samuel 18:8–11 says, "And Saul was very wroth, and the saying displeased him; and he said, They have ascribed unto David ten thousands, and to me they have ascribed but thousands: and what can he have more but the kingdom? And Saul eyed David from that day and forward. And it came to pass on the morrow, that the evil spirit from God came upon Saul, and he prophesied in the midst of the house: and David played with his hand, as at other times: and there was a javelin in Saul's hand. And Saul cast the javelin; for he said, I will smite David even to the wall with it. And David avoided out of his presence twice."

I could not for the life of me understand why God would give anyone an "evil spirit." Similarly, the scripture says God gave Pharaoh a "hardened heart" against Moses and the people of Israel.

Exodus 11:9–10 says, "And the LORD said unto Moses, Go in unto Pharaoh: for I have hardened his heart, and the heart of his servants, that I might shew these my signs before him: And that thou mayest tell in the ears of thy son, and of thy son's son, what things I have wrought in Egypt, and my signs which I have done among them; that ye may know how that I am the LORD."

There it is—God allowed evil and a hardened heart, so that the people would know that God was the Lord. In Moses' case and in the case of David, I believe he was still proving his purpose and it's fulfillment.

Through the righteousness of David, God continually allowed David to escape the judgment and condemnation of King Saul. The Bible states that David escaped Saul each time he tried to kill him, because of the evil spirit that came upon Saul. What I am saying is that purpose may not always be what you prayed about, or even a call you may understand, but you must keep on moving. The way to do that is through prayer. Remember, your purpose starts with your prayer life. Yes, purpose is a call on your life. Everyone has a call to purpose.

Praying has brought me through some really bad times in life—times that I just didn't want to go on in a purpose or in my life or my ministry or my church or anything. But when I stopped by the throne of grace, my thoughts and attitude would change.

Smile with me right here. Just in case you really have prayed and prayed and things are still in circular motion, you must break the cycle. To do that, keep giving it to God. Don't stop! You may not understand it right now, but that's alright. You may be in a place of not understanding, but God always understands.

Start with prayer for your purpose, ladies and gentlemen. When you start talking to God about it, you show your connection and, I promise you, you can never go wrong with being a God-connector. Your purpose starts with a real prayer life. Amen.

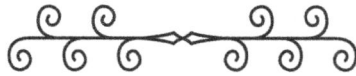

Pray This Prayer for the Start of Your Purpose through Prayer

Oh Lord, what would I do without being able to talk with you about me? You placed in me a desire to pour into the world around me—a purpose that I know could have only come from above. In spite of my gifts and callings, I will pray to you about everything and all things will work together for my good. I know that all things in life's purposes may not be understood all the time, but I trust you so much. I love you so much and I want your purpose to make my life alive. I vow to pray about it all to your glory, honor, and praise. In Jesus' name I pray. Amen.

Chapter 6

Power, Purpose and Revelation

Ecclesiastes 3:1a—*To every [thing there is] a season, and a time to every purpose under the heaven.*

Galations 1:12—*For I neither received it of man, neither was I taught [it], but by the revelation of Jesus Christ.*

Revelation brings power. So what is the connection between power and revelation? I was having a conversation with someone concerning some small things that had been laid on my heart and the more I began to share, the more I began to realize that what was actually happening was that I was receiving a higher revelation. I was being instructed in knowing who I was, and what I was purposed to do in my life, for God was about to take me to another level spiritually in him. I hadn't seen it before, but it was revealed through simply sharing in conversation. So I just began to write more and more and seek out the power of God through wisdom, in order to ensure the right pathway.

Perhaps this book may not reveal anything "new," to you, but my prayer is that it may cause you to share with someone else—someone who may need just a little encouragement in discovering their powerful purpose. Please enjoy and be blessed in your purpose for this moment in time. So, the word *purpose* is something that someone intends to get or do; an intention or an aim; a resolution or a determination; it is the object for which something is done and there is an end in view." Amen?

To have a set purpose means that you are functioning with a specific end in view and that whatever you set out to do, it is not accidental but by design. It is deliberate and it is by God for you. Sometimes it is easy to begin with the question "why?" Why am I here on this earth? Why do I exist? Why was I born?

The simple question "why?" may stem from one thing, and that one thing is in the knowing of one's own purpose and power in life...as it has been predestined by God. The question "why?" applies at all stages and ages, so let's talk about it.

Asking questions can be very good but they can also be hurtful to people who really do want power or purpose, especially if both power and purpose have been hindered in the past. There have been times in my life where I have had to ask if I may have missed God, or possibly even missed my season. Such questions and thoughts are painful, because deeply embedded beyond heartfelt emotion or logic of the mind or the root of the soul, everyone wants to know the special purpose and power God has for their lives.

Though it is true we are special because he created us in his own image, at times we can still ponder why we even exist. The answer to these questions are revealed through prayer and in the Word of God.

If you mean to truly know the "why," seek counsel and use wisdom, and you will be blessed to find the answer to your power and your purpose. Go a little further and even prioritize a fast and all will be well; in other words, be prepared to go out deeper. The soul (mind, will, and emotions) hold three components that cause a person to consistently ask the question "why."

If you really want to know of the special purpose God has for your existence, ask him. It's that simple.

In my personal revelation, I do know and believe that this book's purpose was given to me as an assignment by the Lord, in which I thought would only be a dream if I ever published it. I truly believe God has placed this assignment into my hands, to write for the sole purpose of giving him the complete glory and to help people find their powerful purpose. Thank God, I have been instructed to direct my focus on knowing and touching the lives of people.

Revelation is a part of preparation for anyone who desires to experience kingdom purpose and to be a powerful being in the kingdom. I start with God's revelatory purpose out of personal conviction. I believe that if you knew what the creator of mankind intended for you at the start, then some of the jealousies, envying, backbiting, sadness, thoughts of suicide, failures, defeated attitudes, and depression would be revealed to you for what they really are—distractions!

I believe that with revelation these distractions would not have such a stronghold on anyone, especially those who claim to know the Lord, because once a thing has been revealed you can and will be healed and walk in you powerful wealthy place of purpose…on purpose! I know that every revelatory purpose must go through some ups and downs in order to be perfected. In order for the accomplishment that God has set for it, you must have and expect a revelation. I have even heard people say that they were "pregnant" with a ministry or vision/purpose.

Does that mean something profound to you? Are you expecting? Yes, expectation is powerful…it is a place of un-birthed purpose. When you are pregnant, you are still holding something until the appointed time, vision or purpose to be brought forth, birthed, revealed, and released.

When I first came to Christ over thirty plus years ago, I immediately began to sing on the church choir. I never prayed and asked God to reveal to me if this was the area I should operate in, as it pertained to the revelation of my purpose or in my life, or my ministry, or my church or anything. It never dawned on me that the reason I didn't ask God for direction was that I knew as well as others that I had a gift and just simply began to operate in it. God's power on display…Amen.

I was only eighteen years old when my music ministry began, though it never crossed my mind as to whether the Lord had purposed me to go in the direction of gospel/inspirational music. I believe that my decision in continuing with the church was because I enjoyed that type of singing, but still I had not received the revelation as too whether this was the ministry of purpose for me.

Honestly, it seemed to me that I was either asked to participate in a particular ministry or did so from interest. I was touched by the Lord, given the anointing to accomplish the assignment and then just carried out the mission for service. Whether I would teach, direct the choir, sing a solo, sing background, or give a soul stirring fellowship—just to fulfill the powerful purpose of God, and in allowing myself to be used was my focus and mission. The purpose and the plan seemed to go simultaneously hand in hand; this was revelation and God's power in process.

You may not need to look for a ministry or service because whatever you are doing right now in life you have been doing and could be your final destination of a right-now purpose. If you are married, work a job, are a parent, or serve in some other capacity in life, this could possibly be your final revelatory purpose and ultimate God given power on display...Halleluia.

Accept it, for it is in those things or that one thing that you are purposed to do in your life and in this season. Start somewhere and God will do the rest. Just have faith. *Matthew 25:15-18, and 29 says, "And unto one he gave five talents, to another two, and to another one; to every man according to his several ability; andstraightway took his journey. Then he that had received the five talents went and traded with the same, and made them other five talents. And likewise he that had received two, he also gained other two. But he that had received one went and digged in the earth and hid his lords money. For unto everyone that hath shall be given, and he shall have abundance: but from him that hath not shall be taken away even that which he hath."*

Whatever talents you have been given by the Lord, take them and use them. Then pray about other areas where God can use you and how. Get ready to walk in this newly revealed power, through God in you.

The "how" happens by simply getting involved and staying sensitive to the leading of God Almighty. Some purposes do not involve serving in a church setting; it may be that you are called to serve in some type of secular area of employment. My point is to show that in every person's life, there is a revealed position of purpose and the power to fulfill it. The gift of revelation is so essential to the place of your purpose and you must find it. When you do nothing with your life, you will not experience *real* life. Be open for the move of God, and don't fret. Go forth with trust and belief in the Saviour, Jesus Christ. Go with the flow of God, Amen?

I do believe that changes in assignments are primarily directed toward everyone's purpose. Self-examination may be very much a part of this manifestation or revelation.

Simply move with the cloud like the children of Israel did, as they traveled through the wilderness in search of Canaan. When the cloud of God's provision and covering moved, so did they—complaining the whole way, but moving. By asking yourself questions in the natural and allowing discernment in the Spirit, it will help in determining what your particular purpose may be. What do you like to do? What gifts and abilities do you possess? Go to www.SpiritualGiftsTest.com and take the test to see what your gifts may be. To do this is a powerful move toward self-awareness.

John 15:14–16 says, "Ye are my friends if ye do whatsoever I command you. Henceforth I call you not servants; for the servant knoweth not what his lord doeth: but I have called you friends; for all things that I have heard of my father I have made known unto you. Ye have not chosen me but I have chosen you, and ordained you, that ye should go and bring forth fruit, and that your fruit should remain: that whatsoever ye shall ask of the Father in my name, that he may give it you."

My point from this scripture is that we should look at ourselves as more than just servants, but as friends of the Lord. "Bring forth the fruit, then ask me for whatever you want.

Better yet, ask the Father in my name, for in my name he (the Father) will do it for you . . . my friends."

Again, God says, you are now my friends and there are no more secrets concerning what it is that I have ordained you to do. You are ordained to serve God—what a powerful revelation!

Ordaining is another very powerful way in which God says I have authorized, predestined, or invested in you. The Lord's primary concern here is that we bear fruit that will last and become purpose fulfilling.

While you are seeking direction toward the ministry/purpose that God has chosen for you, pray, get into doing daily devotionals, and participate in personal or group Bible study, Sunday school, and regular church services. Get spiritually involved, connected, and educated.

Now we are getting to the meat. Notice I said meat and not milk because, the bible refers to meat as being for the seasoned believers and milk for the beginners. Seek his will for your life and don't waste your time running here and there for answers.

There is a revelation from God to you. Spend a good amount of time in personal study of the Word, fasting, praising, and worshipping and then begin to watch miraculous things happen to you. I did, and now I'm writing about it. Amen.

God will give you new revelation and enlighten your desires. You will find that God himself will take into consideration your personality (meaning all of who and what you are), and as he begins to develop, grow, and join you with the vision he has prepared, the beautiful gift of revelation and power will begin to bloom. The end result can only be one of complete gratification and blessing.

It's a bit like going to school for years, just so that in the end you will be able to perform in that particular area and place of study. For years, you can study, prepare, and grow, so that at the time of graduation you will be able to present yourself as the best in that particular field. You can build up in knowledge, yet after that comes the real work. That is called the revelation of application.

After recognizing that where you are in life right now is your present season of purpose, you can begin to thank God for this revelation by simply moving forward and applying obedience while you perform it. For God will not give you something and not allow you to be empowered and effective in it (and by "it" I mean what he has ordained for your purpose). Investing in you is called self-empowerment, and this is his purpose, and he expects a testimony declaring how wonderful he is, through his power that works in you.

If he sends you to the north, south, east or west, believe me, he knows what he is doing. Hallelujah!

God sent Abraham away from his familiar place of habitation, away from the place surrounded by family, friends, and even his place of worship. I'm sure Abraham did not understand God's profound move on his life at first, but **Genesis 12:1–2 says, "Now the Lord had said unto Abram, Get thee out of thy country, and from thy kindred, and from thy father's house, unto a land that I will shew thee: And I will make of thee a great nation, and I will bless thee, and make thy name great; and thou shalt be a blessing."** As we see, the end result, was one of complete excellence. The story of Abraham shows the obedience and faith of a man, who next to Christ, should be followed. We can show something similar to our own family, friends, co-workers, and mates by following the divine plan and destination of a right-now purpose of God...putting him on full display.

Why is it that the very move of God is sometimes so misunderstood? Could it be because God needs to cleanse and change us, so that our thinking can be on the same page with his? *Philippians 2:5a says, "Let this mind be in you, which was also in Christ Jesus."* My final thought on power, revelation and your purpose is that we should all take serious and deep thought, about all of our reasons "why," and what we are doing or have sought to do for purpose manifestation. God will reveal all in due season. Amen?

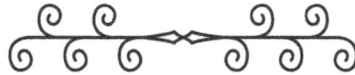

Pray This Prayer for the Gift of Revelation and Power in Your Purpose

Thank you, Jesus, for revealing to me the gift of revelation while I pursue my purpose.

God, I thank you for being so personal to me, for keeping your hands on my needs, especially in the area of my gifting. Continue to open me up as I surrender myself, and pour into me revelation that will help me every step of the way. In Jesus' name I pray. Amen.

Chapter 7

Fulfilling My Purpose by Persistence

James 1:18—*In fulfillment of his own purpose he gave us birth by the word of truth, so that we would become a kind of first fruits of his creatures. (NRS)*

Will I always care about the fulfillment of my purpose? Will I always love serving and sacrificing for the God? Due to the essential need of clarity for purpose fulfillment and persistence, the answer to this question I have learned can only be experienced by questioning God, his word, and the right people. Because any questions for clarity show maturity and focus in the person asking. Let me talk to leader's right here. How many know that without effective leadership, there lies room for confusion and a lack of productivity.

Of course, everyone can't be a leader; there has to be followers. There is only one God; there was only one Moses; there was only one Paul. I think you get my point. If people in leadership are hindered, those who follow may be hindered too and not be persistent in fulfilling a purpose. Fulfillment is not just for those in leadership. There are those who work in the background, and sometimes people just don't want to fulfill the goal, the dream, and the assignment. We all get discouraged from within, meaning within our ministry and within ourselves. When things don't go our way, we can feel inclined to quit and not to persist. This allows the enemy of our souls to provoke us out of wanting to serve the Lord and fulfilling his purpose.

Some of those symptoms come in the disguises of personality battles, clashes, poor communication, power struggles, politics, personal cliques and preferences. All of that is foolishness of the flesh, and these behaviors only hinder and distract the work of God being fulfilled.

Throughout the Bible we see this happen. If not dealt with properly through godly leadership, this "only the strong survive" mentality can and will pose serious hindrances in ministry and life.

Leaders, please pay attention to this: The enemy fights you, people will fight you, and spiritual warfare will rise up from places you may never have expected. All of that is just to keep you from being persistent in pursuing and fulfilling your purpose. Although you may be in a position of high visibility or status in ministry, remember that *Luke 12:48 says, "For to whomsoever much is given, of him shall be much required."* Be spiritually sensitive to those who are following you as you follow Christ. Let's try to remember who this is all about: Jesus.

As I went about to fulfill my purpose in church service, I realized how much we all need one another. If

God is to use us in the fulfillment of our purposes, we must be open and humble and persistent. Fulfillment of purpose and the role of leadership is so powerful if done right. It's powerful because leaders are to be the example setters, especially to those who are sensitive or new in the faith, for they can be discouraged and quit. Those who are not in leadership should try to respect the line of authority, for this is God's divine order. Granted, excellence is expected, from and for all. The Lord expects excellence for he is a most excellent leader and wishes all to have fulfilled their purpose. Again, excellence must be a part of you. Pray and ask God to give you his anointing, and I promise you he will do it.

Let's not get lost in the fear of the words "expectation, excellence and perfection." **Matthew 5:8 says, "Be ye therefore perfect, even as your Father which is in heaven is perfect."** Yes, we can strive for what we are not. In spite of the challenges in purpose fulfillment, we are to be faithful, available, and teachable (F.A.T). We are also to be thankful, and thankfulness will help you along the pathway of experiencing the persistence, needed for fulfillment of the purpose God has for you. Thankfulness puts the cherry on top of the cake. It should happen at the end of each miracle, sign, or wonder of God. But at the end, the goal should be to realize fulfillment.

Let's take a closer look at F.A.T.:

FAITHFUL: To show a strong sense of duty or responsibility, constant, reliable and loyal.

AVAILABLE: Someone who can be used; one who is strong and willing.

TEACHABLE: Someone who is able to be instructed, developed, and provided with knowledge and skills.

To be fulfilled in the Lord is joy. Fulfillment in your purpose should be joyous, and to be fulfilled means to be satisfied and complete, this will only happen if you go after it. Of course, life and ministry may not always make you feel the most joyous, satisfied, or complete. Nevertheless, it is good to know that the Lord will still bless, and fulfillment will be your experience—but only if you keep on pushing and being persistent.

David speaks concerning his trials in purpose, and in *Psalm 55:5–8, he says, "Fearfulness and trembling are come upon me, and horror hath overwhelmed me. And I said, Oh that I had wings like a dove! For then would I fly away and be at rest. Lo, then would I wander far off, and remain in the wilderness. Selah. I would hasten my escape from the windy storm and tempest."* Sometimes in life while trying to keep a balance and focus on things, we sometimes just want to get away, hide, and escape. We want to escape from pain; from tiredness; from being held responsible; and from the same old routine. Can I get a witness? Praise God! We want to escape from the stormy winds and those violent elements that stem from a plain old (boring) simple life. Can I just keep it really real!? **Psalm 55:5 says, "Fearfulness and trembling are come upon me, and horror hath overwhelmed me."**

David admits that it is his own fears and feelings of horror that have come upon him and that if he could just be free like a bird and live in the wilderness, he might be able to rest. Don't we all feel like that at some points? We just need some rest...we feel block and stuck. This is why we need to be filled with the Holy Spirit in order to fulfill that specific purpose given to us. You see God is well capable; it is you and I who must remember who, whose, and what we are. Let's be honest: Without him it will be completely impossible to fulfill a purpose or even pursue it. For though we may have abilities and manifold gifts, our assigned purpose may be more than our human capabilities can handle. The way through is to pray and ask God for spiritual strength and then rest, trust, and rest even more. There is no such thing as a superhero. The only hero is God, and his almighty power found in the name of his son Jesus.

Remember, fulfillment is carrying out your purpose persistently, which is more than just receiving a check or hearing the words thank you. It should be the joyous experience of knowing that you did something great that brought glory to the name of Christ. It was his anointing that empowered you and made you effective, not any power of your own solely. "God only" is my fulfiller, my rock, my defense, my refuge, my strength, and my glory. Hallelujah!

Staying connected to God is the only way to be excellent in the fulfillment of purpose and more than just a survivor in this life. I know that most of what I am saying has been taught in church, so this is just a friendly reminder.

Ephesians 6:11 says, "Put on the whole armor of God, that ye may be able to stand against the wiles of the devil."

The fulfillment of the purpose commandment is that we put on the whole armor of God. By doing this, we may be able to stand against the wiles of the devil. Even if you have experienced church hurt, you can get over it…I did. Never allow anxieties, or any other negatives to stop you, for they will come. Just relax, take a deep breath, and go for a jog or a walk if you have to; but whatever you do, go straight to God with your dilemma, be persistent an NEVER give up. *I Peter 5:7 says, "Casting all your care upon him; for he careth for you."* This is a learned behavior. Casting your cares is a required behavior for purpose fulfillment.

May I also say that I have found soul winning to be thee most fulfilling purpose filler of all, and I know everyone that has accepted Christ as his or her personal Lord and Savior can be a witness to the saving of souls.

Who wouldn't want to see someone in their own family saved due to some seed planted, or even by some testimony that was given. Let me tell you, when I was going through trials, I would witness to people when I didn't feel like it. I would just go ahead and witness. Just try it. I encourage you to tap in and at the next opportunity, give a testimony of what God has done in your life, and give it as if it were your last time. Allow yourself to be completely used in turning that person's life around. Amen? Making a person aware of how much God loves him or her and cares is such an awesome ministry within itself.

Seeing a challenged life transformed can be such a fulfillment to purpose. This should be the goal of every believer.

So be in prayer about this purpose filler called "soul winning." Yes, I'm am biased toward soul winning.

Bringing fulfillment to a person's life by being persistent not pushy and in guiding them to the fulfiller himself, is the most awesome experience. Trust me when I tell you this.

Proverbs 11:30 says, "The fruit of the righteous is a tree of life; and he that winneth souls is wise." And Galatians 6:9 says, "And let us not be weary in well doing: for in due season we shall reap, if we faint not. So as stated before going forth, remember."

You now have a new name, why not fill in the blanks and confirm it!

_____ *'Purpose Fulfiller'* _____

Your First Name   **Your Last Name**

Pray This Prayer for Fulfilling Your Purpose with Persistence

*Halleluja*h Lord! I glorify your name above all and everything*! Thank you for equipping me and teaching me how to serve* in fulfilling my purpose with conviction and persistence.

As I go forth to discover and to seek your face in total submission to your Holy Spirit, may the fulfillment of souls be won for the kingdom, and may humility and persistence be in the forefront of fulfilling my purpose. Help me to be different from the world that this work may be done in excellence. I glorify your name! In Jesus' name I pray. Amen.

Chapter 8

Fasting and Praying for My Purpose

Ezra 8:21—*I proclaimed a fast there beside the Ahava Canal, a fast to humble ourselves before our God and pray for wise guidance for our journey—all our people and possessions. (The Message)*

In my personal life when challenged with the obstacles of seeking God for direction and dealing with change, the one thing I consistently do is fast. Now fasting has never been a preferred area of spiritual sacrifice for me, I'm sure there are others who would agree. I would always turn to fasting when I felt the hindering power of the enemy working on me through my flesh. I absolutely believe that fasting does destroy demonic spiritual strongholds.

Praise and worship breaks strongholds too. Amen? Christ declared to his disciples in **Matthew 17:18-21:** *"And Jesus rebuked the devil; and he departed out of him and the child was cured from that very hour. Then came the disciples to Jesus apart, and said, 'Why could not we cast him out?' And Jesus said unto them, 'Because of your unbelief: For verily I say unto you, if ye have faith as a grain of mustard seed, ye shall say unto this mountain, Remove hence to yonder place; and it shall remove; and nothing shall be impossible unto you. Howbeit this kind goeth not out but by prayer and fasting.'"*

We can always fast for direction. **Acts 13:2–3 says,** *"As they ministered to the Lord, and fasted, the Holy Ghost said, Separate me Barnabas and Saul for the work whereunto I have called them. And when they* *had fasted and prayed, and laid their hands on them, they sent them away."*

Here, the Holy Spirit directed them to separate Barnabas and Saul for the work. It is true that for the purpose of God to be fully manifested in you, a separation may need to take place. Spiritually appointed seclusion may be very much needed (just for a season), so that you may be able to hear from the Lord. There are many types of fasts. Personally, I recommend a study of the Word concerning the various types and ways of fasting, or you could consult a minister, elder or counselor from your church home for a Bible-based fast. If you are under medical care, check with your physician.

The world has various types of fasts and they may be similar to the fasts found in the Bible. The object is to be taught and guided correctly by God in how to fast and pray. Incorrectly applying biblical principles will surely defeat your purpose, and since this book is about you,

God, and purpose, I want to encourage you to stay on track. Along with fasting, we must pray. Seal everything with a prayer, for prayer is a direct line of communication between you and the Lord. Yes, he is Lord, I said **HE** is the Lord. This is my declaration. Will you make it yours? Now you may have already heard many of the things that I am saying before, so I may be repeating the things you already know. But it's not always the knowing that counts, but it is what you do with the information received.

It is the doing that causes life to be productive and effective. Many miss the mark by not applying God's principles through his written word. Amen. Applying prayer is so important because when you pray, you acknowledge that you need a higher source of help and direction. This can only come through prayer to the almighty God, Jehovah- Jireh (the Lord God My Provider).

Matthew 21:22 says, "And all things, whatsoever ye shall ask in prayer, believing, ye shall receive." And

Romans 8:26 says, "Likewise the Spirit also helpeth our infirmities: For we know not what we should pray for as we ought: but the Spirit itself maketh intercession for us with groanings which cannot be uttered."

At times, we simply get tired of waiting, hoping, trusting, and even of praying itself. Can I be real and can I get a witness? This is when we must fight. Use the Word, be determined and be diligent, yet most of all fast and pray about it. The scripture also says in *Romans 12:10-11, "Be kindly affectionate one to another with brotherly love; in honor preferring one another; Not slothful in business; fervent in spirit serving the Lord.*
That word fervent means to be fired up... on fire... burning super willing to serve."

Every day we see people go to and fro, working in their respective places of employment, and at the end of the two week working period, that person has an expectancy. That expectancy is to receive a paycheck. Well, this should be the same for those who fast and pray for the manifestation of purpose in life. Our frame of mind should be to expect manifold blessings.

Though these things be a reasonable service, our expectancies should be deeply rooted in the Lord. *Jeremiah 29:11 says, For I know the thoughts that I think toward you, saith the Lord, thoughts of peace, and not of evil, to give you an expected end."* As a result of our fasting, praying, and obeying, there is the end result of expectancy.

As we fast and pray, we can have the same kind of anticipation that parents of an unborn child do. We need the joy of expectancy, excitement, and jubilance over what the Lord is about to do in our lives because we have turned our plate down and humbled ourselves through prayer.

Just know that as that unborn child is being developed inside the womb of the mother, so it should be when it comes to our expectancy for our purpose. Growth and nourishment both take time. God must feed us, purge us, and prove us. His purpose is to take us to a higher place in him, transporting us from the carnal to the spiritual. In other words, from glory to glory to glory. The Lord is preparing, moving, testing, trying, and rearranging.

We are to be the head and not the tail; we are above only. Though it may not feel like it at times, we are *never* beneath! Let's look at a word of confirmation. You may begin to ask yourself (as I often have) what you are the head of and what you are above.

The Bible states that we who stand in God stand in a place of spiritual authority, which means we are above every condition, every circumstance, every situation, and every attack that may come our way— whether these things come from Satan or from bad decisions. God has given us the gift of power, through his written word, over everything. The Lord has made you the possessor, so go in and possess.

Put on the frame of mind of the possessor and start with a good fast and begin to seriously seek God's face through prayer, for one hour, one day, or one month—whatever you are led to do.

There is an old song I used to sing with the choir named *"There's a Bright Side Somewhere."* Whoever offers praise, glorifies God. So offer to the Lord the sacrifices of praise, a broken spirit, and a contrite and broken heart, which actually for some, means a humbled spirit. Offer to him yourself completely that he may completely use you for his glory.

The purpose of absolute relinquishment of one's own will can and will be a blessing to the Lord. *Psalm 55:17 says, " Evening and morning, and at noon, will I pray and cry aloud: and he shall hear my voice."* While you are on your fast and in prayer, do as the scripture above states, and keep on praying.

Do it in the morning, in the noonday, and in the evening—all day long. Keep in mind that some have the philosophy that all you have to do is ask one time and then wait. If that is what you wish to do, then your praying once is enough for you. But some people need to tarry and keep seeking until they feel a peace or experience their miraculous purpose and breakthrough. Remember, Christ prayed three times in the Garden of Gethsemane.

Romans 14:5b says, "Let every man be fully persuaded in his own mind." Expectancy for your purpose and enlightenment for "your" purpose begins with self-denial. In order to see the bright side, we must sacrifice and come out of our comfort zone (yes I had to do this too), because self-sacrifice is a vital part of purpose and breakthrough. Strongholds are brought down through your fasting and praying.

Prayers bring the power of God shows to the Lord how serious you are about getting the direction and answers concerning your purpose. Fasting means you deny your own self-will and relinquish all to the Lord and to the glory of his Lordship. Here are a few more scriptural examples of men and women who after fasting saw great moves of God or were given divine instructions.

The first was in **Jeremiah 36:5–6—"And Jeremiah commanded Baruch, saying, 'I am shut up; I cannot go into the house of the LORD: Therefore go thou, and read in the roll, which thou has written from my mouth, the words of the Lord in the ears of the people in the Lord's house upon the fasting day: and also thou shalt read them in the ears of all Judah that come out of their cities.'"** Jeremiah instructs Baruch to read the law on the day that the children of Israel are fasting in order that they may be given divine instruction to live anew in God.

On a personal note, have you ever noticed that while you were on your fast, every type of temptation for food seems to come your way? Or while you are in prayer a thought may come across your mind to throw you off. This is the enemy. These are his distractions, but the Word says in *Isaiah 54:17, "No weapon that is formed against thee shall prosper; and every tongue that shall rise against thee in judgment thou shalt condemn."* Can I get an Amen? I once heard a Sunday school teacher put it this way; "If your mind wanders to something while praying start praying on that thing that just came to mind."

I so agree with that because the point is to never lose focus. Just don't give the enemy any props. You can go forth and believe now! Yes, go forth and grow in God. Grow in the manifold blessings, of completing your fast and make sure to keep on praying, alongside. Whether it be one hour, one day, or forty days, just know that something good is going to happen to you and miraculous blessings will come your way! Praise God!

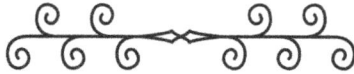

Pray This Prayer as You Fast and Pray For Your Kingdom Purpose

Oh Lord, I bless your name. I thank you Jesus for causing me to see how important it is that I yield to fasting and prayer in seeking for my purpose. You have shaken up the places that were keeping me bound by the enemy. You, Lord, have helped me to turn my plate down and you have taught me how to pray and what to say. I worship and bow down to you. In Jesus' name I pray. Amen.

Chapter 9

Healed and Ready for My Purpose

Luke 6:18—And they that were vexed with unclean spirits:
and they were healed.

A broken heart and spirit must be healed in order
for your readiness for purpose to come to fruition. To be
ready means to be prepared for an immediate,
spontaneous, and prompt use. So no matter what it looks
like, or even how it may feel, remember the Lord will work
his miracles in your life. He alone is the healer; he is the
potter and we are the clay.

The Bible states this and we should humble ourselves
to this truth found in the Word. *Jeremiah 18:6 says, "Oh,*
house of Israel, cannot I do with you as this potter?
Saith the Lord, Behold, as the clay is in the potter's
hand, so are ye in mine hand, O house of Israel."

The Lord will always show us the straight and simple paths in life that lead toward success. Even now I am working on coming off of hypertension medication and diabetes medication. When I first started this book, I was younger and did not have the same challenges, but I do have them now and I declared the victory through it all and to come off of them all. This is what we must do. In other words, you have to do what you have to do. He wants us to not only reach our Canaan land, he wants us to possess it! It's all up to you! Say yes to possess!

The healing and readiness that must take place in your life can be a blessing and not some unwanted burden. David said in **Psalm 16:8–11, "I have set the Lord always before me: because He is at my right hand, I shall not be moved. Therefore my heart is glad, and my glory rejoiceth: my flesh also shall rest in hope. For thou wilt not leave my soul in hell; neither wilt thou suffer thine Holy one to see corruption. Thou** *wilt shew me the path of life: in thy presence is fullness of joy; at thy right hand there are pleasures for evermore."* Praise God! In being healed, we must ask for deliverance from any and all hurtful feelings. This is a major part of our readiness. Emotional healing is always a big challenge because it deals with the flesh. Here again comes that familiar word *soul*. The soul consists of the mind (the thinking), the will (the decisions), and the emotions (the feelings).

Once we release those old strongholds that come through the door of our defeated and fleshly ways, then we free ourselves to let the healing begin and get the healing we need. Deliverance from people is so very crucial. I am still learning this! The influence of others, the opinion of others, the expectations of others, and the manipulations of others must be dealt with in a healthy and spiritual way. If you haven't thought about it this way before, please consider that all who may be in your life and in your face, may not have your best interest at heart.

Let's look at a few of these words a bit more closely to back up what I am saying as it connects with people dealing with people: Influence can be good or bad. Influence means to effect the condition or development of something or someone.

Opinions can also be a positive or a negative. Opinion means to have a belief or to hold to a conclusion with confidence, but not substantiated by positive knowledge or proof.

Expectations can be encouraging or discouraging. Expectations are eager anticipations of others or self. Manipulation/ is always a negative. Manipulation is shrewd or devious ways, especially used for one's own advantage.

Influence, opinion, expectations, and manipulation are all a part of life, so watch and pray at all times. Be aware of your spiritual surroundings. Always be forgiving and praying, and always be ready to repent. Always go back to the Word, no matter what people say or do, for in this way you cannot go wrong.

There is a song that I have often sung with the praise team entitled "I Am the God That Healeth Thee" by Don Moen. (You can listen to it on YouTube.) The healing is in Him (Jesus Christ), and it is in his word, for Jesus is the Word. And you will find (as a friend once told me), when people begin to act up in the spirit, speak the Word on them and watch the effect. See the change in the situation and behaviors once the Word is spoken. Amen. All that I could do from that advice was kind of laugh to myself, because it actually was true. Amen.

Listen, keep lifting up the Word, for the Word will bring about a change, correction, and humility, especially if spoken with power and clear authority. The enemy of the Word may try to debate, pushing you to doubt and argue.

Believe me, through all of that, it is God who will have the last word. Amen. Now that we understand the obstacles and triumphs of the healing process, what part do we actually play in this? The answer is surrender. Yield to the spirit of God, let him in and let him heal YOU. Allow the healing to make you over again; take off the old and start with the new.

Mark 2:21–22 says, "No man also seweth a piece of new cloth on an old garment: else the new piece that filled it up taketh away from the old, and the rent is made worse. And no man putteth new wine into old bottles: else the new wine doth burst the bottles, and the wine is spilled, and the bottles will be marred: but new wine must be put into new bottles."

A new mind, a new talk, a new walk, and a new way of living are God's purposes for everyone. Whatever your race and background, he wants to make you new and ready for what you were born into this world to do! Your destiny and purpose belongs to God, and he will give you the power to fulfill it. You must make a decision. Ask yourself if you are healed and ready. You are here for a reason, and that reason is not for you to die or to be in a dead state of mind, unfruitful and lifeless. Amen.

Many times in the past, the thought of suicide came into my mind and heart. I was experiencing adversity and confusion and didn't really know how to deal with it. But I am still here and delivered. Thank you Jesus! If you are fighting with thoughts of suicide, giving up, and letting go of your dreams and hope, please STOP! Turn to God and hear his voice through this book today, because purpose is calling you.

Through praise, worship, and speaking the written word against these strongholds, I escaped and received total deliverance. When I felt as though I wanted to end it all, I honestly believed it would be better to be home with the Lord than suffering here on earth. I battled these thoughts and feelings for years. This was clearly a serious case of demonic influence.

Though I survived this, it did take its toll on my perception of life in general. But, I kept on praying, fasting, and growing until one day, when adversities came, I decided I didn't want to take my own life anymore. I just began to really go berserk (crazy and radical) in my pursuit to get to God because I really did want to live.

When the battle was on, I would try to remember those militant gospel song selections that I would sing with the choir. I never stopped crying to the Lord and asking in prayer. I never stopped going to church (though I felt like it, believe me). I never stopped being involved, despite the challenges I had with people and myself, and I never stopped fellowshipping with the saints. **Praise the Lord! I am still alive! Healed and ready for my purpose!**

Some things only come through growth. Allow the growth process to be birthed in you. If you've made the decision to receive your healing and you are truly ready to be released from your past, then you have made the first and most important step.

Philippians 3:14 says, "I press toward the mark for the prize of the high calling of God in Christ Jesus." The past is the past; the future is the future. In order to press forward, there must be a release. Release the past and press toward the future for the sake of purpose. This is pleasing to the Lord, for this is his plan for our healing and readiness.

On a more personal note, through various means (reading the Word, hearing a song, or through some preaching), I realized there were still some areas that I needed to pay close attention to in my spiritual growth. Pessimism and how I perceived things affected my way of thinking about myself, my past, my former marriages, family situations, educational problems, and some shattered dreams and expectations. Although I still had some serious adversities to deal with through my growth process, I didn't understand a lot of things concerning my new life with Christ. My desire to smoke, drink, and club were in direct competition with praying, faith, hope and going to church. Again, staying involved and focused helped me through. I also must give credit to my mother who for those first years of my new life with Christ, was there to apply good godly guidance despite my resistance. It was she, who after much searching, found a place for my family to worship (my brother and I). Later in life my dad would lay his hands on my head and pray for me, which was precious and special for me.

I pray that all families can come together and worship in a healthy way as mine did. A life without Christ is a great big challenge, and one that no one should have to face.

Now that I am confessing my own healing and readiness, I can only pray that the Lord will continue to show me more and more areas that need to be healed and made ready for the purpose he has called me too.

I am at the point in my life where God is about to birth a ministry through me, for it has been confirmed through the mouths of many as well as in my heart. The blessed thing about the Lord is that when he calls you, he needs no one to speak a ministry into your life, for he will reveal it to you first and foremost and then confirm it. As I am about to embark upon a new horizon of purpose, I still have to remind myself of *II Timothy 1:7—For God has not given us the spirit of fear; but of power, and of love, and of a sound mind.*"

We all must stand in a place of needing a healing touch from God, and whether already being used by God kingdom purpose or not, anyone who is at least willing to love God enough to try, is a battle halfway won!   Go into your Canaan land, healed and ready for your purpose. *Romans 8:1 says, "There is therefore now no condemnation to them which are in Christ Jesus, who walk not after the flesh, but after the Spirit."*

According to Bishop J.D. Corbett (2010), "Believers must guard against self-condemnation because of the sins of the past, mistakes in judgment, bad decisions or failed projects. Negative opinions of others toward you can also cause condemnation in the heart. Thinking that you have let others down brings condemnation. Feeling like you have failed God is probably the greatest cause of condemnation of the heart." For years I lived under the thumb of self-condemnation. My anger kept me from dealing with my shortcomings and failures in a healthy and spiritual way, and of course this hindered my readiness for purpose.   It took me a long time to realize that I don't have to be liked by everybody. Instead I was emotionally affected by the unkind things that people said about me.

Anger was another major hindrance to my readiness and healing for purpose. I did pray, and I kept going to church, but it was a real battle. Even preparing for the ministry call was a whirlwind of emotions. I thought I was so strong, but what I was really doing was holding everything in and hiding my emotions—and becoming more bitter and angry. I started to not like people at all.

Obviously, this was a hindrance to my readiness and healing for my purpose. Low-self-esteem and anger were hindrances to my readiness and healing. So next in line was me for the purpose of needing to be healed. Hurting and hurting others is normal for those who need to be healed, and that was me. Nothing wrong with calling on God, but I had to encourage myself not to put people (the people I claimed not to like) in the place of equality with who God was to me.

To choose to pursue healing, I had to ask myself these questions: Do I want purpose to be fulfilled? Do I want to be healed? Do I want to be ready?

My word of encouragement today is to make a decision. If you want to be healed and ready for a purpose in life, you must decide, prepare, and connect with God. There is only so much your family (church and non-church), friends, pastors, and others can do for you. They didn't create you, so, remember, people are limited. They may intercede on your behalf in prayer or even touch and agree with you in prayer. Remember it is God who is in totally control, not man. In essence, just know that the Lord looks at you. *Ephesians 3:20 says, "Now unto him that is able to do exceeding abundantly above all that we ask or think, according to the power that worketh in us..."*

There is power that works in us. Yes—you have power! If you are a person who was raised to be a certain way and you find your responses to issues of life being nonspiritual and disconnected from God, this is dysfunctional and deserves your attention. There is no need to blow your witness due to some of these challenges in everyday life.

When you go through challenges, pain, and trials, it hurts if you hear someone say, "It's not that serious." It can seem insensitive.

But throughout the Bible, God provides us with guidance about the steps that should be taken and choices that should be followed. If we do the Word, things won't be that serious. Give God a chance to fix you! He can do it! Be encouraged by some of these scriptures.

I Peter 5:7—"Casting all your care upon him; for he careth for you."

Mark 11:23—"For verily I say unto you, That whosoever shall say unto this mountain, Be thou removed, and be thou cast into the sea; and shall not doubt in his heart, but shall believe that those things which he saith shall come to pass; he shall have whatsoever he saith."

Proverbs 18:21—"Death and life are in the power of the tongue: and they that love it shall eat the fruit thereof."

Mark 11:22-25—"And Jesus answering saith unto them, 'Have faith in God. For verily I say unto you, that whosoever shall say Unto this mountain, be thou removed, and be thou cast into the sea; and shall not doubt in his heart, but shall believe that those thing which he saith shall come to pass; he shall have whatsoever he saith. Therefore I say unto you, What things soever ye desire, when ye pray, believe that ye receive them, and ye shall have them. And when ye stand praying, forgive, if ye have ought against any: that your Father also which is in heaven may forgive you your trespasses."

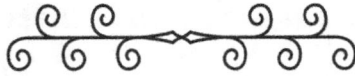

Pray This Prayer to Be Healed and Ready For Your Purpose.

Lord, thank you. Thank you for healing me in my broken places. I release my brokenness to you and I ask you to completely heal me and make me ready for my purpose. I pray this prayer to you only.

Father, please remove every part of bitterness, unforgiveness, and anger that have prevented my deliverance and healing. I praise you and me thank you in Jesus' name. Amen.

Chapter 10

The Power of Self-Sacrificing for Purpose

Leviticus 22:29—*When you sacrifice a sacrifice of thanksgiving to the LORD, you shall sacrifice it so that you may be accepted. (NAS)*

Have you ever made a vow to the Lord? You may have been in a situation where you felt that your back was against the wall, and you said, "Lord! If you get me through this one, I'll ----" Or "Lord! If you get me out of this, I promise I will never do that again." Can I get a witness? At that very crucial point in your life you made a self-sacrificing vow. You vowed that if you were rescued from the pressure, the trial, the point of death, or the compromise that you would not look back.

Once you made this self-sacrificing vow, you entered into an agreement with yourself and God to take on an action. At that point in your life, you were ready for your position to transition, and from the point of transition, you were hoping that it would bring about a new power in self-sacrificing purpose. Realize that before the power of purpose can be revealed, you will need to be put in a place of self-sacrifice. You may have vowed to be obedient or to live out a godly testimony or to be a witness that God could use. Let's face it, there are many things that we don't want to endure, things that test our rights and freedoms, but we deal with these things and move forward with the right decisions because our lives may depend on it...yes it is a sacrifice.

Even the everyday routine of life can be self-sacrificing. But we must be unselfish, vow keeping, and self-sacrificing. We all have to make sacrifices for God,

Self and others. What are your sacrifices? What are you are involved in that is outside of your comfort zone? Are you a willing vessel? Do you feel powerful by it or weakened?

It is not just enough to just surrender your will to the Lord in spite of your opinion and personal feelings. You must be a true self-denier and self-sacrificer for godly power to be displayed in your purpose. From my experience, I have concluded that until we learn to humble ourselves and do things the way God intends for it to be done, then we will have to face those same challenges again and again. I don't know about you, but if there is a way to avoid redundancy, I am all for it. Amen? You see, self-sacrifice by definition is the act of giving up something or someone willingly. Now how many are truly willing to give up and give in for the cause of the purpose? Self-sacrifice in your purpose will only be a blessing if done with the right frame of mind and spirit. In spite of the issues that you may have to face, never forget that self-sacrifice is a vital key to kingdom-building purpose and power. So let me ask you the million dollar question, what are you needing to sacrifice today? Food, drug use, wrong friends etc. The power comes when you can really let it go.

The prophet Samuel put it this way when he began to upbraid (rebuke) Saul for his disobedience: ***"And Samuel said, Hath the Lord as great delight in burnt offerings and sacrifices, as in obeying the voice of the Lord? Behold to obey is better than sacrifice, and to hearken (listen) than the fat of rams" (1 Samuel 15:22).***

Although it is true that God wants obedience, in this context, sacrifice is defined as "excuses." The point is clear: Don't allow your sacrifices to be used as excuses; be obedient and listen (hearken) because listening and obeying is better than a burnt offering or telling God how much of a vow you have made and how much you have sacrificed.

If the thing you are sacrificing causes you to be disobedient, then STOP! You can never be frustrated with God's divine will of self-sacrifice because obedience is the power that holds the hand of self-sacrifice for your purpose. Amen.

Pray This Prayer for the Power of Self-Sacrifice in Your Purpose

Yes, Lord! Thank you for being Lord, and for teaching me how to be unselfish in my quest for purpose.

Thank you for walking me through and showing me that it is not all about me. I surrender my selfish ways and my own philosophy. Guide me by the power of your Holy Spirit that is filled with wisdom, to the place where obedience and self-sacrifice are connected in my life's purpose. Amen.

Chapter 11

Proverbs 3:5–6 Purpose, Power, Persistence & Prayer

Proverbs 3:5–6—*Trust in the LORD with all thine heart; and lean not unto thine own understanding. In all thy ways acknowledge him, and he shall direct thy paths.*

The understanding of the heart is so crucial when it comes your purpose. What does your heart tell you? Will your heart trust him? Is it telling you to lean not unto your own understanding? Is it telling you to acknowledge him, and is it telling you to allow him to direct your paths?

As people of faith, we have to decide whether we will allow God to be God. We are here on this planet for a reason and the reason for the believer is to give God the glory. We are to honor him, bless him, and worship him He is awesome. There is nobody like the Lord. If all he asks of us is to trust, lean on, and acknowledge him, we should push toward that goal with all godly determination and with all of our might. Being in the spirit of good cheer is a great place to be in your quest for the Proverbs 3:5-6 purpose. Things in life are serious enough and through the many circumstances that may come your way, you must remember what Jesus says to his disciples: *"Behold, the hour cometh, yea, is now come, that ye shall be scattered, every man to his own, and shall leave me alone: and yet I am not alone, because the Father is with me. 33-These things I have spoken unto you, that in me ye might have peace. In the world ye shall have tribulation: but be of good cheer; I have overcome the world" (John 16:32–33).*

Remember, God is a bottom-line God, and the bottom line where God is concerned is that he is the one who has overcome the trials, tribulations, stresses, challenges, doubts, disappointments, sorrows, heartache, weaknesses, and everything else. You name it, and the Word will show you how God overcame it and that He did it for you and I.

Though the enemy of your purpose wants to frustrate your purpose, doesn't mean he has to win. Remember, you are never alone. You are a winner in Christ Jesus! God will visit you with peace, but you must surrender your non-peaceful, non-trusting feelings to God. Sometimes we just don't feel very spiritual and one thing we know for sure is that tribulation comes. It is a part of being alive and human. Nothing is perfect. Things happen. Don't be a victim to the abuse of the negatives. God was with Jesus as he died on the cross and God the father will be with you!

We ask, "How long Lord? How long?!" But Proverbs 3:5-6 people of purpose can trust Him and never doubt. You may wonder how long you have to do that, and the answer is as long as it takes. It took me a long time to learn this, but some things take so long in our purpose because God knows the end result.

We have to be prepared for the purpose. We have to pray, fast, and then pray and fast some more. Trusting and having faith in the invisible is our job. Purging and preparing is God's job. He is Lord!

I am reminded of the hymn "Trust and Obey." I love the hymns, they hold so much power. Proverbs 3:5–6 people, it is your time and this is your season to walk in the newness of your life and in the purpose of trust. Come alive in your purpose! Proverbs leads you to a way in God where you can never go wrong. I really mean that. I have lived and continue to live it, each and every day of my life. Speak life to yourself according to the written word…walk in your miracle…talk in your miracle…believe in your miracle…hope for your own future and watch God's Proverb 3:5-6 purpose come alive in you!

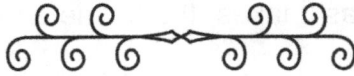

Pray This Prayer for the Proverbs 3:5–6 Purpose

Oh, Lord, I praise you and I bless your awesome name! How great is our God! My soul magnifies the Lord! Father, cause me to be a person who will walk, talk, and breathe your written word for my life. Build my faith walk in you and fill me with your Holy Spirit. I want to do all that a person would do who believes in the Proverbs 3:5-6 purpose. I admit that I cannot do it by myself. I stretch out on your word through faith. I wait to see the end result and I celebrate in God's bottom line in my life. I promise to acknowledge you, because it is in you that I will trust for my direction, and my personal pathway. Oh Lord, again I praise you! I praise you, I praise you, and I trust you. In Jesus' name I pray. Amen.

Chapter 12

Overcome Purpose Challenges and Adversities
with Prayer

Isaiah 30:20

[20] And though the Lord give you the bread of adversity, and the water of affliction, yet shall not thy teachers be removed into a corner any more, but thine eyes shall see thy teachers:[21] And thine ears shall hear a word behind thee, saying, This is the way, walk ye in it, when ye turn to the right hand, and when ye turn to the left. - KJV

Challenges to our purpose come from different directions: from Satan, from our very selves, and from the Lord for purposes of our testing and growth. For starters, let's talk about Satan being an instrument of our adversity.

Satan himself will come in many disguises and for right now, we will just address him as the Adversary. He loves to come into your pathways with various distractions and disguises. He may come into your place of employment; your personal relationships; your finances; your family; and your church.

The adversary may be a challenge to these areas of your life from time to time, and God may allow that in order to test and to grow you as a believer. The blessing in this is that God is the Supervisor and when you pray to him, even while going through…he hears and will answer in due season. That means if you are a born again Christian, Satan can only go so far. **John 10:10 says, "The thief cometh not but for to steal, and to kill and to destroy, but I have come that he may have life, and that he may have it more abundantly."**

The Adversary attacks and this is why these three components of man must be held with great sensitivity. As I said earlier in the book, these areas reflect the component of the soul and they are:

1. The Mind—Thinking, which means the way we see things.

2. The Will—Decisions, which means the way we react to things.

3. The Emotions–Senses, which means how we feel about things.

These three areas make up the soul, the real you, so while the Lord is trying to use you, and to lay a foundation in you through his Holy Spirit and by his written word, the adversary's job is try to prevent you, block you, and stop you. Now that you have this information, it is up to you to RESIST! Self-inflicted, non-resisted temptations are the number one source of bad decision making.

God has provided an antidote for you, and that antidote is forgiveness and help through the power of prayer. We all make bad decisions, and God knows our weaknesses, so just know that with his help, you can become immune to all of the demonic forces, feelings of inadequacy, insecurities, and any other negative emotional or physical attacks—if you resist them.

Let's just keep it real: Decisions that are not spirit led can cause you to be thrown off track permanently and hold back your season of blessings in God. Through your adversities exercise the power of prayer and stay in communication with the Lord. He is your strength and empowerment. Respond to adversity with faith, prayer, faith, prayer, faith and more prayer! Stay in the written word and keep his purpose, because no matter what trials come, they are only for our own empowerment. Remember, ***Romans 8:28 says, "And we know that all things work together for good to them that love God, to them who are the called according to his purpose."***

Your bad decisions may hurt a little, but if you hold on to God and put prayer on it everything will work in your favor. He must get the glory, and, yes, things and people may sometimes hurt you, but respond with prayer…cry out to the Lord. He will help you to overcome.

But how many know we can be our own worst enemy. How? Through weaknesses within and by allowing the flesh, to make you feel as though you are not received or loved; this could be determined as a "self-inflicted lie." Push back the drama and the emotionalism, and watch the end result.

The connection is to remember to TRUST GOD. My point is to stress that there will be some distractions, challenges, and adversities, and you must guard yourself with the Word of God and prayer. Guard your heart and your purpose for from there you will find that you just cannot lose. No matter what path(s) you may have traveled, you will and can overcome challenges/adversities and be successful. Amen.

Adversities do not discriminate. No matter your age, race, , financial status, blood-family line, challenges will find you. Nevertheless, know that the love of God is immutable (meaning without change), and he will send protection to your side—yes, even an "angel.*"*

Psalm 34:7–8 says, "The angel of the Lord encampeth round about them that fear him, and delivereth them. O' taste and see that the Lord is good: blessed is the man that trusteth in him." Never depend on the comfort and approval of man when dealing with overcoming your bad decisions. God by himself will help you…too help yourself. If you are seeking confirmations concerning a purpose or a mission, then I strongly suggest the application of prayer, faith, and works. Stay involved in your heart's passion for ministry and for life.

Be encouraged that God will only allow challenges when he needs to get your attention, grow you in some area, or move your flesh in order that his Spirit may take control. Godly challenges in your life are not always bad.

Those challenges may not feel good, but in the end, they may do you a world of good. ***Proverbs 4:7 says, "Wisdom is the principal thing; therefore get wisdom: and with all thy getting get understanding."*** And ***Ecclesiastes 3:1 says, "To everything there is a season and a time to every purpose under heaven:"***

This tells us there is a time when there will be no adversities and then a time when there will be adversities, but know that God allows these challenges to perfect your purpose.

How you respond to your challenges will either cause you to come out victoriously or remain a victim to your tests and trials. As ***I Peter 5:10 says, "But the God of all grace, who hath called us unto his eternal glory by Christ Jesus, after that ye have suffered a while, make you perfect, stablish, strengthen, settle you."***

Stay with the lord! Let him handle your adversities and your enemies, and, finally, let him handle YOU and your purpose. In the end everything will be alright, but you must pray!

***

Pray this prayer for purpose through your challenges/adversity

Oh, heavenly Father, thank you for every challenge, trial, test, and all adversarial tactic. Forgive me for being my own stumbling block. Lift me up above all of my own folly. Protect me from the adversary and break all strong holds. Lord, every test and trial that comes my way, I pray that you will perfect me through it. Make me, mold me, and teach me how to be an overcomer in pursuit of my divine and blessed purpose. In Jesus' name. Amen.

Chapter 13

The Power of Purpose and Your Money

1 Timothy 6:10—*For the love of money is the root of all evil which while some coveted after they have erred from the faith and pierced themselves through with many sorrows.*

__Money, money, money!!! Debt...debt...debt!!! Free...Free...Free!!! You know there is a little cliché spoken in some churches that state, "Everybody talking about heaven aint going there." Well, this little cliché can humorously be repeated..."Everybody talking about money isn't getting any. Whew! What a shocking revelation right? Wrong. This plight of financial wealth and well being...meaning, being debt free, is what many would call a plight and an unfair challenge. Scammers, schemers, shammers and flim flammers...in other words... con artistry runs rampant when you are hungry.

So let's cure this starvation. Let all calm down and realize that the answer starts with you! Will you take those self-sacrificing steps, toward purpose for your money. If you are faith based, you should be the type of person who holds onto scripture principles, for dear life. If you are not faith based...faith based application may not be you route. Here is where we separate the men from the boys, and the women from the girls...finally the poor from the rich. Somebody say, MONEY- PURPOSE, POWER, PERSISTENCE and PRAYER! What is the purpose for your money and how do we find out that answer? I have watched many run to and fro, in order to short cut their way to financial wealth, and then attach God as if to seal the deal. Many including yours truly, have not wanted money to be hard to come by. Simply put, most of us just don't want to work hard for the money, but we want the money. We come across as hostile, angry and judgmental toward faith based leaders who focus on prosperity. Yet the church is expected to rescue those at the first of the month, when rent is due. We are to expect prosperity but when a faith base leader rises up with a little too much wealth, we all complain and state foul play. We don't want our faith based leaders with multimillion dollar homes or personal jets and nice state of the art cars or land. Or should I say we don't want it to be too visible. For those who do not know, those faith based leaders of the Bible were wealthy and their wealth was said to have come from God...yes, heaven above. For every person who reads the chapter of this book, let me say that I know we will all have to agree to disagree with some of what I am saying, because where money is concerned, people are simply divided...so sad but true. Those of the faith have been accused of wanting to receive and giving very little in comparison (ask those in music ministry). I mean maybe a card, candles, chicken dinner, and some flowers (most things purchased very inexpensively) from your local neighborhood dollar stores for one dollar. Can we keep it real, in comparison, God gave his only son, and the son gave his life at the cross. Why such sacrifice, this sacrifice was due to God, and his son acting and knowing that the price, that needed to be paid for the debt of sinful man, deemed a price worthy of a priceless life. So, should we be hostile and all out cruel because a few of us prosper, or ask for help to prosper and achieve it?

There is a need for change. If you are a person who believes in prosperity and change...now is your turn to please stand up. People, people, people...YOU can walk in purpose, power, persistence and pray through with YOUR money! Want to hear something funny, I remember hearing sermons preached, where those who heard the scripture chapter and verses, for that sermon, would actually play the scripture chapter and verses as apart of the daily lottery number (gambling and not going by faith). The purpose was in hope of hitting the number and winning easy money...wow right? Let's keep it real...cause on top of that, if you were faith based and believed in tithing, it was told to be ok, to expect a tither to pay their tithes to the church out of the lottery winnings...how funny and sad.

Ecclesiastes 10:19 says, "A feast is made for laughter, and wine maketh merry: but money answereth all things."

Yes, money answers all things people...money answers everything. Did you hear that? What does that mean to you? What that means to me, is that I need to tap into the purpose and power of MY money, persistently and prayerfully! Will God bless your money...sure he will, and show you how to grow it too. I am growing mine right now, how? By empowering you through this book...Amen.

Isaiah 48:17 says, "Thus saith the LORD, thy Redeemer, the Holy One of Israel; I am the LORD thy

God which teacheth thee to profit, which leadeth thee by the way that thou shouldest go."

Yes, yes, yes, God can teach you how to profit, there is an education that you can acquire from God concerning your MONEY. It starts with education, and ends with obedience to that education. So, where does this education start? It starts with biblical principles…yes, doing it God's way. Your purpose for God and your money, is calling on you. Now whether you want to walk in super wealth or just to be comfortable, will be determined by how purpose will show up in your money.

There are of course many opinions about how much money is enough and how much money is too much. At this point I am not attempting a debate but just offering some food for thought. Why, because education about a thing removes ignorance of the same. Kingdom purpose and your money must have a relationship. The relationship that these two have, will only be a blessing and not a curse to you…if you hear and obey walk in the power of it by persistence and pray…pray…pray! Become a doer and not just a hearer, hire a financial consultant; do or attend a workshop at your local church or business. There are even several non-profit organization that get funding for helping those in the community, who need that extra support, but may not have the funds. Bottom line, your money has a purpose, established a long time ago. Yes, God had you in mind; God has your money in mind...now it's your turn to put both on YOUR mind.

Now it is time to celebrate, although some may tithe and some may not. The scriptures state that every man should be persuaded in his own mind.

Romans 14:5 says, "One man esteemeth one day above another: another esteemeth every day alike. Let every man be fully persuaded in his own mind."

I love the way God does things in his education, he

leaves choice. Today let the choice be yours in order to receive the "fat of the land." Do it God's way is my encouragement. Why, because purpose is calling you and your money. Legal pursuit of wealth building is key, so decide how you want to build wealth and walk in your established wealthy place...multimillions or just be comfortable.

Pray This Prayer for Money in Your Purpose

God you are the almighty God who is omniscient, omnipresent and omnipotent, meaning there is nothing in my life that is seen as too hard for you. I desire to increase my money, I desire to be wealthy and live off of the fat of the land. You are a God of provision and I thank you for providing for me. If there is any area in my finances that I have not surrendered,

I ask for your forgiveness and ask you to take control of me and my financial understanding. I am above and not beneath. I am blessed in the city and in the fields, laying down and standing. I am a lender and not only a borrower. I am your child and I do thank you for the victory of having my money speak purpose...All these things I pray in your name...Amen.

Chapter 14

Victory in Purpose, Persistence, Power and Prayer

*2 **Chronicles 20:27**—Then they returned, every man of Judah and Jerusalem, and Jehoshaphat in the forefront of them, to go again to Jerusalem with joy; for the LORD had made them to rejoice over their enemies.*

God's end result for his children of purpose is victory! He wants the world to know that his people are victorious.

II Corinthians 2:14 says, "Now thanks be unto God, which always causeth us to triumph in Christ, and maketh manifest the saviour of his knowledge by us in every place."

Be thankful unto God and rejoice because we never are without victory, nor are we without the knowledge and victory we have in Christ Jesus....WE WALK IN POWER!

In other words, we should not walk around ignorant of victorious living. **Psalm 37:4 says, "Delight thyself also in the Lord; and he shall give thee the desires of thine heart."** We will have our desires fulfilled—this is thevictory. Our dreams will come true—this is our victory. Your righteous heart's desires will come to pass! I want to make note of the word *also* in this verse. This word lets us know that God sees, that there are other things in life that we may want to delight in, and he just wants us tofirst and foremost, "delight in Him." He sort of allows himself to be an attachment and humbly offers the benefitof giving to us the desires of our heart.

If we would just attach him and make him an "also," part of our lives, we will experience the powerful right-nowvictory!

When we were in the world—meaning behaving and living our lives separate from God—the enemy used us, abused us, and hindered us. Our enemy did this so that we would be blinded from our God-given purpose and our coming victory in that purpose. If it had not been for the disobedience of man (Adam and Eve) in the Garden of Eden (see Genesis 3), we may not have been separated from God, and who knows how things would have turned out. But God in his omniscience (all knowingness) saw past all of our shortcomings and failures and sent his only begotten son, Jesus, to give us the victory. *I John 5:4–5 says, "For whatsoever is born of God overcometh the world: and this is the victory that overcometh the world, even our faith. Who is he that overcometh theworld, but he that believeth that Jesus is the Son of God?"*

We can pray in victory realizing that we are overcomers because, being a believer in the Son of God, automatically makes us overcomers. This means that you also automatically have the victory in your life and ultimately in your purpose. Victory-Nike (Nee-Kay) is a Greek word that means "conquest or the means of success" (Strong's Exhaustive Concordance). Can you image going through life unsure and without really knowing what your purpose may be in this life and in God? Can you imagine not being successful at anything?

There is a story in the Bible about such a young man; his name was Joseph (see Genesis Chapters 37, 39, and

40). After Joseph dreamt a dream of success asa ruler, he found himself in a place of failure. One minutehe was in a prosperous place, and in the next minute he was in a desert place. At one point he was with his family, and in the next he was a slave in Egypt. At one point he was thrown in a pit, then he was in a palace. Promoted and then demoted, back and forth. Another man who went through the same challenge but in a different way was Job. Job had everything and then losteverything all in one hit. In the end he gained it all back.Through all of their ups and downs, the end result for these two men was seen through the eyes of Victory!

Make the declaration of victory your song of praise today and every day. God can and will make a way out of no way, but you really must believe it—and you really must believe in him and in the power of his mighty hand.

The scripture talks about this in the form of having faith in God. Now keep in mind that God does know what he is doing when it comes to you. The scriptures state that before we were born and while we were yet in the womb, God anointed us with a victorious purpose.

Jeremiah 1:4–6 says, "Then the word of the LORD come unto me, saying, 'Before I formed thee inthe belly I knew thee; and before thou camest forth out of the womb I sanctified thee, and I ordained theea prophet unto the nations.' Then said I, 'Ah, Lord GOD! Behold, I cannot speak: for I am a child."

Although God is speaking here to Jeremiah, the message should be clear for us all. It means, you are **ordained** with victorious power and purpose! Look at the above text. It shows the transparency of Jeremiah and how he ended the text by acknowledging his inability, his inadequacy, his shortcomings, and his weakness.

Nevertheless, God still called him, knew him, sanctified him, and used him! Hallellujah! Victory in this man's purpose is written all over him. Don't underestimate God. Believe him even when it doesn't make sense and just wait things out and see what the end result will be. It's what I'm doing right now with some things that I am facing. We all have to do it. I believe the key to experiencing the victory is in knowing who you are and whose you are. Who are you? Do you know? I know that I am Trinita Renée Lattimore and, I am a St. Luke 1:37 woman! I know I am a minister, singer, musician, friend, sister, aunt, daughter, and counselor/coach. I know that although I am single and enjoying, I do hope for marriage one day etc.

I know that I trust and believe God above all. But as far as purpose is concerned, I need to ask the reoccurring question: what am I supposed to be doing with my life?

Just because I am using my gifts and talents, does that mean I am operating within the ordained purpose, power, persistence for my victorious purpose and the power that accompanies it? I have been a soloist for years, and when I gave my life to the Lord, I joined a localchurch, and I immediately began to sing. As time progressed, I began to do more and as I got older, more of my gifts and talents began to surface. From self- examination I have concluded that I am multifaceted andlove to do all with excellence. It seems that if I put my mind to an idea and began to plan to do a certain thing, Iam able to convince others to pray for and believe with me. Don't get me wrong, I have messed up along the way, but that happens. The point is that we are striving for perfection, yet we haven't arrived there yet.

If you can relate to what I am saying, don't beat yourself up over past failures. Victory still belongs to you!Do you know who you are and whose you are?

1 Peter 2:9 says, "But ye are a chosen generation, a royal priesthood, an holy nation, a peculiar people; that ye should shew forth the praisesof him who hath called you out of darkness into his marvelous light;"

What do you feel that you really want to do in this life? I mean outside of what you may have gone to college or trade school for. Have you prayed about it? Have you done any research into it? Have you talked to others whoare already doing it? The goal should be for you to be victorious. You were given power to do it…so let's get to it.

Success is yours but you must know how to approach it. I like *Proverbs 28:20, which says, "A faithful man shall abound with blessings: but he that maketh haste to be rich shall not be innocent."* Don't be in a rush. Slow down or God will slow you down. God isthe one who ordained your purpose from the womb, so don't be quick to use it for a get-rich-quick plan. Just be faithful and watch God enrich you with long-term blessingsand satisfaction. He will and he can. Can I get an AMEN?

Once you have found the answer to all of the questions that anyone with real desire for purpose would ask, it is now your turn. Yes! Your turn. Look at *Hebrews 11:6: "But without faith it is impossible to please him: for he that cometh to God must believe that he is, and that he is a rewarder of them that diligently seek him."*

No matter what the end result for you and your purpose may be in this life, just know that Christ Jesus is there and that spells "V-I-C-T-O-R-Y!" Marriages may fallapart; families may be on the decline; finances may be insufficient; friends may be few. But through it all, you cantrust. Just learn to trust! He is well able to finish his assignment through you and give to you a powerful, purposeful, persistence and prayer filled life of VICTORY.

Remember, some things he will do for you, but most things he will do **through you**. Victory today, right now, is mine. Speak it by the written word in faith, and then believe it!

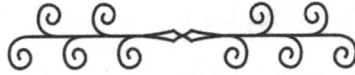

Pray This Prayer for Victory in Purpose, Power, Persistence and Prayer

Thank you, Lord, for victory! I bless you and I praise you! Lord, I desire to live a powerful victorious life and I want my purpose, power, persistence and prayer life to be of great victory. Fill my life and purpose with victory. Through this prayer may othersalso experience the victory that comes with having a personal and strong spiritual relationship with you. I love and I praise your name! In Jesus' name I pray.

Amen.

REFERENCES

Corbett, J.D. 2010. Senior Pastor at Greenville Community Christian Church and Pastor at Greenville Community ChristianChurch

Henry, M. (1706). Ecclesiastes. In *Matthew Henry commentary on the whole Bible (complete).* Retrieved from http://www.biblestudytools.com/commentaries/matthew-henry-complete/ecclesiastes

http://library.timelesstruths.org/music/Trust_and_Obey/ Webster's dictionary. Retrieved from http://www.merriam-webster.com/dictionary/divine

(Acts 13:2–3, King James Version)

(Galatians 5:22, King James Version)

(Genesis 1:26–27, King James Version)

(Genesis 5:1. King James Version)

(Genesis 12:1–2, King James Version)

(Ecclesiastes 3:1, King James Version)

(Ephesians 3:20, King James Version)

(Ecclesiastes 8:6, King James Version)

(Ephesians 1:11, King James Version)

(Ephesians 3:7–11, King James Version)

(Ephesians 6:10, King James Version)

(Ephesians 6:11, King James Version)

(Exodus 15:20, King James Version)

(Ezra 8:21, King James Version)

(I Corinthians 2:9–10, King James Version)

(I Corinthians 6:9–11, King James Version)

(I Corinthians 6:20, King James Version)

(II Corinthians 2:14, King James Version)

(I John 3:8, King James Version)

(I John 5:4–5, King James Version)

(I Peter 5:7, King James Version)

(II Chronicles 20:27, King James Version)

(II Timothy 1:9–11, King James Version)

(Habakkuk 2:2, King James Version)

(Hebrews 11:6, King James Version)

(Hosea 4:6, King James Version)

(Isaiah 54:17, King James Version)

(Isaiah 14:26, King James Version)

(Isaiah 30:20–21, King James Version)

(Isaiah 54:17, King James Version)

(James 1:18, King James Version)

(Jeremiah 1:4–6, King James Version)

(Jeremiah 18:6, King James Version)

(Jeremiah 29:11, King James Version)

(Judges 6:11-39–11, King James Version)

(Leviticus 22:29, King James Version)

(Mark 11:22–25, King James Version)

(Philippians 3:14 King James Version)

(Proverbs 4:7, King James Version)

(Proverbs 20:18a, King James Version)

(Psalm 8:4–7, King James Version)

(Psalm 55:5–8, King James Version)

(Romans 8:28, King James Version)

(Romans 14:17, King James Version)

(Luke 6:18, King James Version)

(Luke 10:11, King James Version)

(John 16:32–33, King James Version)

(John 10:10, King James Version)

(Matthew 17:18–21, King James Version)

(Matthew 12:28, King James Version)

(Matthew 17:18–21, King James Version)

(Matthew 25:15–18; 29, King James Version)

(Luke 11:18–20, King James Version)

(Luke 12:48, King James Version)

(Luke 13:18, King James Version)

(John 15:14–16, King James Version)

(I Peter 2:9, King James Version)

(I Peter 5:10, King James Version)

(I Samuel 15:22, King James Version)

(II Timothy 1:7, King James Version)

(Titus 2:12, King James Version)

(Titus 3:4–7, King James Version)

(Philippians 2:5, King James Version)

(Philippians 3:14, King James Version)

(Psalm 16:8–11, King James Version)

(Psalm 37:4, King James Version)

(Psalm 37:23, King James Version)

(Proverbs 3:5–6, King James Version)

(Proverbs 4:7, King James Version)

(Proverbs 11:30, King James Version)

(Proverbs 18:21, King James Version)

(Proverbs 28:20, King James Version)

(Proverbs 31:10–31, King James Version)

(Revelation 21:6, King James Version)

(Romans 8:1, King James Version)

(Romans 8:29–30, King James Version)

(Romans 12:1, King James Version)

(Romans 10:9–10, King James Version)

ABOUT THE AUTHOR

Trinita R. Lattimore

*Elder T.R. Lattimore
*Gospel/Inspirational Psalmist
*Licensed Professional Counselor-Supervisor
*Certified Life Coach *Speaker and Author

Elder Trinita R. Lattimore also endearingly called Elder T, is a native of the Washington, DC area. She gave her life to Christ at the age of eighteen. Elder Elect Lattimore is a passionate, inspirational, people empowerer, helper and advocate. Her goal is to direct people toward self empowerment and a successful life in their faith, through a connected relationship with God.

THE MINISTRY SCRIPTURE – Trinita Lattimore's ministry and life scripture is: St. Luke 1:37 - "For with God, nothing shall be impossible." Her personal declaration is: "I AM A ST. LUKE 1:37 WOMAN!"

THE MINISTRY - Elder- Trinita. R. Lattimore, declares freedom to live the gospel; freedom to preach the gospel; freedom to teach the gospel and freedom to sing the gospel…to the glory of God. She has been a gospel/inspirational psalmist for 30 plus years...and has on occasion worked in radio as a talk show co-host and executive producer. She now is a guest Co-host with the Lavonia Perryman show out of Detroit Michigan on iHeartRadio. She was the first Chaplain for the DC Alumni Chapter of Regent University, Virginia Beach, VA. Her focus in the ministry is women, yet her goal is to impact the entire body of Christ.

THE BOOKS - She is the author of a newly published book: Purpose. Power. Persistence. Prayer. and the 30 Day Devotional 'Keeping It Really Real.'

THE FAMILY - Trinita Lattimore attended church consistently and due to the strong encouragement of her mother, the late Sonya B. Ryan (Howard University Alum.), Elder T deems that God has blessed her due to that spiritual legacy. Elder T, is always striving to keep the legacy alive. She is also the sister of Grammy nominated and NAACP Award recipient R&B artist, Kenny Lattimore.

THE EDUCATION - Trinita Lattimore began to prepare for the ministry by receiving her Bachelor's of Biblical Studies from Logos Christian College, Jacksonville, Florida; Masters of Education degree from Regent University, Virginia Beach, Virginia and a Master of Science degree in Clinical and Community Counseling from Johns Hopkins University in Baltimore, Maryland. Finally, she will be attending, Lancaster College\Capital Bible College-- Seminary this fall.

THE MINISTRY SCRIPTURE - Trinita Lattimore ministry and life scripture is: St. Luke 1:37 - "For with God, nothing shall be impossible." Her personal declaration is: "I AM A ST. LUKE 1:37 WOMAN!"

THE COUNSELOR/LIFE COACH - Trinita Lattimore is a Licensed Professional Counselor, Supervisor; Certified Life Coach (C.C.).

Hobbies: Walking, Preaching. Teaching, Singing.

*'LATTYs Creations Handmade Jewelry'

For Ministry Engagements Contact:

<u>Website</u>:
www.trinitalattimore.com

<u>Email</u>:
info@trinitalattimore.com

<u>Social Media</u>:
FB: @TrinitaRLattimore

IG: @trinitalattimore

9 7 9 8 2 1 8 2 4 9 4 8 9